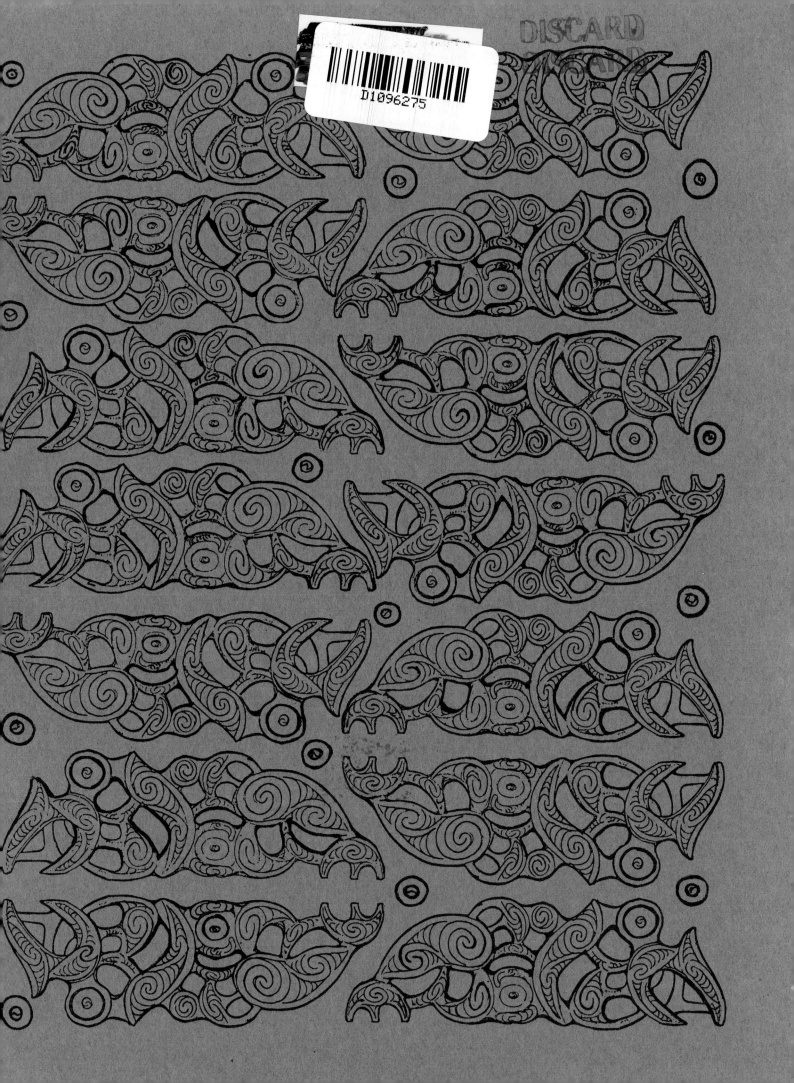

MAORI WOOD SCULPTURE
OF NEW ZEALAND

MAORI WOOD SCULPTURE OF NEW ZEALAND

T. BARROW Ph.D

CHARLES E. TUTTLE COMPANY: PUBLISHERS
RUTLAND, VERMONT & TOKYO, JAPAN

In memory of
KENNETH ATHOL WEBSTER
born in Wellington, 17 December 1906,
died in London, 5 October 1967

Ruia taitea, kia tu ko taikaka anake
Strip away the sapwood, leave only the heartwood
(Maori proverb)

This Tuttle edition is the only edition authorized for sale in
North America, South America, Middle East, and Asia

Published by the Charles E. Tuttle Company, Inc.
of Rutland, Vermont and Tokyo, Japan
with editorial offices at Suido 1-chome, 2–6, Bunkyo-ku, Tokyo, Japan
by special arrangement with A. H. & A. W. Reed, Wellington,
Auckland, and Sydney

Copyright in Japan, 1969 by T. Barrow

Library of Congress Catalog Card No. 79-109412

Standard Book No. 8048 0860-0

PRINTED IN JAPAN

CONTENTS

ACKNOWLEDGMENTS

I ACKNOWLEDGE with all courtesy the help I have had in making this book. I am indebted to authorities in general and museum colleagues, the staffs of universities, personal friends, and private collectors, and I thank the ancient and modern carvers whose creations are the backbone of this work. To the living and the dead I express my gratitude.

Maori friends on several maraes permitted me to photograph houses and carvings, particularly Rongo Halbert of Gisborne, and Pine Taiapa of Tikitiki. Charles I. Tuarau, whom I first met at Centennial Exhibition with Pine Taiapa in 1940, was always helpful. At the Dominion Museum, over a long period of service, I often watched Tuarau at work and thereby gained much practical knowledge.

Some of the friends who encouraged me in my work on Maori wood sculpture are now dead. I think of Ken Webster, to whom I have dedicated this book, W. J. Phillipps, Leslie Adkin, John Houston, and Wattie Carkeek. I cannot remember any men more friendly. I talked with them, years ago, about a massive book on Maori carvings; this modest volume is less than was then aimed at, but I know it would have pleased them.

The book had its substantial beginning in 1963, when I drew on accumulated carving records for the post-primary school bulletin, *The Life and Work of the Maori Carver*, published by the Government Printer in Wellington. The School Publication Branch of the New Zealand Department of Education gave me permission to use any of its materials and text in a larger book, and I am obliged to John Melser, editor of School Publications at that time, for his help.

The bulk of this book was written in Honolulu during a period of research leave away from routine duties at Bishop Museum. For this opportunity to write I thank the Trustees of Bishop Museum and Dr Roland W. Force, Director, as well as colleagues in the Department of Anthropology who were helpful with their interest and co-operation.

The illustrations come from many sources and these are acknowledged individually. I have often taken my own photographs because professional photographers are rarely available when specimens are. My friends George Bacon of Honolulu and George Bull of Wellington are photographers who gave their help freely, especially in the preparation of prints.

Line drawings by Denis Turner were originally intended for *The Life and Work of the Maori Carver,* and to these Vernon King added drawings of similar style. Both artists received photographic reference material with written descriptions of what was needed for accurate visual reconstruction.

The institutional help I have had over the years has directly contributed to the book. As a member of the Department of Internal Affairs and as ethnologist at Dominion Museum I had ready access to collections in New Zealand and overseas. The Maori Affairs Department, and Maori Purposes Fund Board, through the help of J. M. McEwen and W. T. Ngata, were most helpful. Also the members of the Council of the Polynesian Society gave their assistance. In England a grant from the Horniman Foundation allowed me to visit in university vacations many museums of the United Kingdom and Continental Europe; in searching for Maori artifacts I merely touched the surface, yet it was a beginning.

My old teacher Dr H. D. Skinner, Director of Otago Museum, transmitted his enthusiasm to his students, and I have special regard for him as a friend and museum man. My wife Hisako has been devoted to the book, and typed it from a difficult manuscript.

Apart from personal acknowledgments already made I wish to thank those named below for help received: Rigby Allan, G. Archey, W. Allen, B. G. Biggs, I. Bolz, B. A. L. Cranstone, K. Bigwood, R. K. Dell, B. Blackwood, A. Digby, R. S. Duff, G. H. S. Bushnell, R. A. Falla, W. B. Fagg, R. Firth, V. F. Fisher, R. R. Forster, H. Hull, G. Kock, S. Kooijman, P. Ludwig, S. M. Mead, J. S. B. Monro, J. Moreland, W. R. Neill, M. K. Pukui, J. T. Salmon, C. Schollum, F. W. Shawcross, D. R. Simmons, M. Smart, H. Taiapa, B. Teague, E. G. Turbott, C. R. H. Taylor, K. Waaka, A. Wardwell, F. Willett.

For the use of artifacts and other materials from collections both public and private I am obliged to the following institutions and private collections. I have listed to collections the individual items by the numbers which relate artifact or picture to the book. W. O. Oldman Collection items are marked with an asterisk (*):

Alexander Turnbull Library, Wellington: 27, 157, and use of copy of G. F. Angas *The New Zealanders Illustrated* for the plates: 5, 35, 128, 145, 146, 158, 175, 193, 213, 214, 215

American Museum of Natural History, New York: 117, 118

Aberdeen University Anthropology Museum, Scotland: 125

Alexander Museum, Wanganui: 19, 71

Art Gallery and Museum, Kelvingrove, Glasgow, Scotland: 42–43

Auckland Institute and Museum: 13, 14, 15, 16, 47–48, 55–57, 58, 123, 138–141, 144, 154, 160, 180, 184, 197–198, 199, 230–232

K. Bigwood, Blenheim: 194

Department of Anthropology, Auckland University: 20, 67

Bernice P. Bishop Museum, Honolulu: 50, 122, 176

British Museum, London: 32, 70, 72, 73–74, 75, 85, 97, 126, 131–132, 161, 164, 165, 179, 201–203, 206, 219

Cambridge University Museum of Archaeology and Ethnology: 134, 136, 137, 189, 200, 227–229

Canterbury Museum, Christchurch: 17, 18, 130, 163

Dominion Museum, Wellington: frontispiece, 1*, 21, 22, 26, 34, 39–41*, 60, 62–63, 64–65*, 66, 82*, 84, 86–88, 101–106, 119, 129, 133, 174, 182*, 186–188, 205*, 207, 208–210*, 216*, 221*, 223*

Frobenius Institute, Goethe University, Frankfurt-on-Main, West Germany: 226

Gisborne Museum, Gisborne: 98

Hawke's Bay Museum, Napier: 30, 31, 37, 89–92, 149, 224*, 225*

Hunterian Museum, Glasgow University, Scotland: 44, 166

Leningrad Museum of Anthropology and Ethnology, USSR: 99, 100

P. Ludwig Collection: 69

Manchester Museum, England: 162

Montreal Museum of Fine Arts, Canada: 121

Municipal Museum of Ethnology, Cologne, West Germany: 29

Museum für Vlökerkunde, Berlin, West Germany: 83

National Museum of Denmark, Copenhagen: 150, 159

National Museum of Dublin, Ireland: 61, 120

New Zealand Government: The W. O. Oldman Collection was purchased in 1948 then, via the Dominion Museum, shared out to New Zealand museums.

Otago Museum, Dunedin: 23, 24, 25, 33, 151–152, 196

Pitt Rivers Museum, University of Oxford, Oxford: 93–95, 135

Rijksmuseum voor Volkenkunde, Leiden, Holland: 171–172

Saffron Walden Museum, Essex, England: 28

Taranaki Museum, New Plymouth: 76, 96, 124, 156, 177, 178

Tourist and Publicity Department, New Zealand Government, Wellington: 101

University Museum of Pennsylvania, USA: 220

Waitoa Borough Council: 147–148

Webster Collection: 59, 142, 155, 168, 169, 170, 173, 181, 185, 195, 211, 217–218, 233. Many items recorded here are on deposit at the Dominion Museum, Wellington.

INTRODUCTION

THIS BOOK aims at providing New Zealanders and overseas visitors to New Zealand with a selection of some of the finest extant Maori wood sculpture (*whakairo-rakau*). Caption and text together document, as far as available information allows, essential data such as history, measurement, and collection or place where each piece may be seen. Interpretative comment and author's opinion are added to this framework of fact, but the carvings are the most important part of the book. In this era of colour printing it is possible to bring some justice at last to the works of Maori art here illustrated. The muddy old black-and-white plates seen in many early illustrations to Maori art studies did not convey the beauty of the objects.

The Bibliography provides a list of references to literature on the Maori, but specific writing on Maori carving art is scanty. Since Augustus Hamilton's famous *Maori Art*, published in 1896, there has not been available in one book massed material on wood carving although much is scattered through journals, museum monographs, and general books on Maori culture. Generally speaking in existing books the documentation of carvings is either absent or meagre.

This book will allow easy reference on carving to students, art historians, ethnologists, and carvers as well as to general readers.

We are in an age of artistic insight regarding the so-called "primitive arts". Artists in the late 19th century, and today in the 20th century, turned to ethnic arts for inspiration. Some found a special inspiration in the sculpture of Polynesia. New views through anthropology, the books of art historians, television, modern concepts of form and design, and other influences, have opened our eyes to the intention of traditional sculpture and to its remarkable artistic achievements. This book is, in part at least, a contribution to a new assessment of Maori

wood sculpture, as well as a tribute to the Maori carvers whose work is known to the world at large.

If you ask the modern New Zealander, Maori or Pakeha, what aspect of Maori culture he considers its most characteristic production, he is likely to specify wood carving. Wood carving was of primary importance to the old-time Maori, and our national appreciation of it, long dormant, at last seems to be growing. Tourism is a help to the revival of modern wood carving, but Maori pride in the past is also a strong force. The author's hope is that the present book will contribute to a higher standard in modern carving art—whether the carving is a replica for sale, or the panel of a carved house for community use.

The main disadvantage in the study of Maori art, especially to the scholar wishing to study pattern and form, the artist who wishes intelligently to use its motifs, or the general reader merely wishing to enjoy, is simply the lack of well-illustrated books with good descriptive and factual material giving separable analyses and theoretical comment. Also a tremendous amount of rubbish called "Maori art", which is ill conceived and based on the bad imitation of poor carvings, is produced in New Zealand. Plastic models of wood carvings may be acceptable for overseas publicity but even these seem badly conceived. So among other benefits the author hopes this book will encourage all concerned to take another look at what is being done, or misdone, with our wonderful traditional art.

SYSTEM OF REFERENCE AND ARRANGEMENT OF PLATES
Groups of wood carvings generally speaking fall into one or other of two groups: those which result

⇧1   Door lintel (*pare*) of East Coast-Bay of Plenty type.
Dimensions: 43″ (109cm) x 13½″ (34cm).
W. O. Oldman Collection, Dominion Museum, Wellington.

7

2 Captain James Cook, British seaman and greatest of Pacific explorers from the western hemisphere, traded extensively with the Maoris on his several visits to the New Zealand coasts. With his cabin gentlemen and men of the quarterdeck and fo'c's'le, he carried back to England hundreds of "curios" including some of the finest extant carvings. Cook is here depicted in communication with a chief who exchanges ceremonial adze-of-office for a trade axe. The two-handed long club, seen on the right, and the long musket in the hands of Cook's man, were the principal weapons of the time. For obvious reasons the musket soon rendered wooden clubs obsolete. (*Del.* Vernon King)

from group or communal activity such as meeting-house or canoe; and those individual small items which come from the hand of a single carver, e.g., featherboxes, musical instruments, godsticks. Treasure-boxes are the most personal in style and they are also the most difficult to illustrate photographically. Many have six faces with relationship of design extending to all sides. The heads which form end-suspension lugs may have their bodies on the underside.

However, as Maori carving is a thing of the heart rather than of the head, it cannot be classified by any exact system. The Contents List to the book provides a fair guide to the arrangement of carvings but it is necessary to remember that functions and styles must inevitably overlap in certain instances.

All artifacts are listed under the names of museums or other collections in the Acknowledgments. Reference to artifacts and their captions is by continuous numbers from 1 to 233 for every illustration after the frontispiece. Regardless whether the individual photograph is of two or three views of a single object, each illustration has a separate number. Reference numbers are set in bold typeface so they appear heavier and darker than other characters, while a small pointer leads from each caption to its plate in as clear a manner as layout will allow. As text and caption are combined under general subject headings the relationship of introductory text and captions should be self-evident.

Bibliographic reference is provided by surname of the author and year of the publication. The Bibliography itself may be checked for details. No attempt has been made to document the previous appearances of artifacts in the literature, their museum numbers, or the names of successive owners, sellers or donors. Such detail would have called for much more space than can be made available.

DOCUMENTATION

Documentation here extends to significant history, provenience, measurement, and the Maori names of the artifacts. This information is appropriate to the purpose of this book. Because there was difficulty of access to some specimens, such as when museum cases could not or would not open because of jamming or missing keys, it has not been possible in every instance to make first-hand measurements. There were other barriers to easy access as, for example, when reaching a Wairoa stockade post called for an advance across a bull-paddock to a shed, then the hurried excavation of the carving from under several feet of hay while a young Maori girl kept several bulls away with a green switch.

Because of the modern trend to use metric measurements, dimensions are given in centimetres as well as inches, wherever practicable, conversion has been taken to the nearest practical mean. In most cases the measurements were taken by the author but in some instances the measurements quoted have been taken from the literature or from museum records. As dimensions given here are intended to give an impression of size only, they are mostly limited to height or length. Detailed measurements for comparative studies are too complex and specialised for this study, although it is to be observed that the mathematical and computorised study of carvings has immense possibilities as yet untouched.

The paragraphs that precede each subject section are as a rule short introductions to general subjects, while the captions are more specific. With all due respect to authors who have written papers or books which include reference to Maori carvings, to find a particular item often requires an exasperating hunt through book or paper for details of simple measurement, or collection, or history of origin, or other basic information. Often the facts that one wants are just not to be found. The present work is not free of omissions, but an effort has been made to present the material in a systematic order with documentation adequate and appropriate for the scope of the book.

When we look at carving with an analytical eye we should first ask ourselves these questions: When was it made? Where did it come from? What is its regional style? Unfortunately it is rare to find answers on all points. While a carving may have been collected in one region it may have been carved in another, and there is always the danger of inaccurate records. For example, carving which is in the style of one district may have been recorded as having been collected in that district simply on the basis of its regional style.

When we try to reconstruct the picture of Maori art we must start with odd pieces of a giant jigsaw puzzle, but there is some satisfaction in the fact that from a limited number of pieces one can form a general picture. Only a few carvings have been recovered by archaeological excavation and related scientifically to a time-scale based on the measurement of radio-active carbon (the Carbon 14 technique). The truth is that almost all carvings from the earth have been recovered under conditions that would have allowed careful excavation if trained archaeologists had been available. Yet most finds in swamp mud or compacted sand dune have been finds of chance, uplifted by the finder in a rather off-hand way, then left to dry haphazardly or given home "preservation" in the wash-house. A fine Taranaki carving illustrated was found in a ditch by a boy who was looking for a good spot in which to release a discontented pet frog. One of the finest long flutes in existence was sold to Mr Edge Partington in an English jeweller's shop as "the scabbard of a Japanese spear-point". This type of history is found with many of our finest carvings.

Carvings associated with the three voyages of Captain James Cook are especially valuable as they provide a body of data on Classic carving within specific dates. However only some of these carvings can be firmly associated with particular voyages or collectors. Precise place of collection, name of maker and former owner, precise use, the Maori name used at the locality, were never recorded in full. But the picture is not altogether depressing: by careful reconstruction, logical assumptions, and the relating of actual things to old drawings and written

records, and by comparing artifacts in the rich collections of New Zealand and overseas, a tremendous amount of information can be gathered together. We are lucky indeed that Maori carving persisted as a living and transmitted art from prehistoric times to the present. For over two centuries since the time of Cook there have been hundreds of skilled carvers serving the community, and Maori informants have helped in preserving traditional carving lore.

In view of the many gaps in our knowledge of Maori carving, the fragmentary nature of the material itself, and the primitive state of research in this field, it is as yet impossible to fit carvings into exact chronological sequence or to define periods with exactness. An attempt at defining four basic phases or periods is provided at the end of this introduction, but this must be regarded as no more than a basis for further study.

For practical purposes we may use the general theory that Polynesian culture in New Zealand had two phases: the first, termed "Archaic" or "Moa-Hunter", had its beginning with the initial settlement of New Zealand from eastern Polynesia about the 9th century AD, while the second phase is termed "Classic" or "Fleet Maori", and had its beginning before the middle of the 14th century with the arrival on New Zealand shores of many canoes during the last great era of Polynesian sea voyaging.

Many of the sailing canoes from which the Classic Maori claimed his ancestors and to whom even modern Maori attribute their origins, gave their canoe names to the North Island tribes. The old

⇨ 3 Wood carvings in some ways served the pre-Pakeha Maori as a kind of historical record. The images of the great ancestors, which lined the walls of elaborate meeting-houses, were useful when recounting the deeds of notable heroes of the tribe. They also helped to instruct the young, by oral transmission through visual symbols, in the need for resolution and bravery. The lively stories of brave deeds inspired the living, who believed the ancestral spirits watched over the living and that the carved images were their material vehicles. (*Del.* Dennis Turner)

notion of a grand fleet of canoes arriving as a single flotilla has been discredited, but tribal traditions and these canoe names indicate that migratory vessels of substantial size brought well-organised settlers to New Zealand, and not destitute castaways. The Classic phase of Maori life did not come to an abrupt stop with the arrival of Captain Cook and his men in 1769, but this event did mark the end of prehistoric Classic culture and the beginning of a new historic period. In the intervening two hundred years traditional Maori culture has been drastically tried by the impact of western civilisation.

The latter phase may be divided into two periods: the first half is the "Early European Contact" period (1769–1869), and the second half is the "Modern" period (1869 to the present). This proposed outline chronology is arranged in a table on pages 22-3. Observations for each period relating to the life and work of the Maori carver are included under subject headings.

LOCAL STYLES

The adaptation of Maori life over a thousand or more years of Polynesian settlement in New Zealand gave scope to the development of a distinctive carving art which evolved a number of territorial styles. A significant and original analysis of local styles in wood sculpture is found in the article "Maori Art", by J. M. McEwen (see Bibliography). He names the different parts of New Zealand where characteristic local styles evolved and he notes that within each area one must expect considerable variation. There are certain pitfalls that should be avoided, namely the danger of accepting a few similar specimens from an area as constituting a stylistic type when they are in fact the work of one man, and as carvers were great travellers we might expect to find examples of Arawa work in North Auckland, and so on.

The stylistic or "culture" areas are divided by McEwen into two principal groups: the first contains Northland, Hauraki, and part of the Waikato coast and Taranaki, while the second encompasses the remaining parts of the North Island, including of course the notable carving territories of Arawa, Tainui, Matatua, Ngati Porou, Kahungunu, Tuwharetoa, and Wanganui. The absence of extant carving collections from the South Island precludes any analysis of style areas but the existence of thousands of adzes and chisels from southern sites provide abundant evidence that a vigorous wood art once existed throughout the South Island. The line illustrations provided in McEwen's article and his notes on each area are invaluable guides to further study of local style.

4⇨ Wood carvers work on large slabs inside a house at Matapihi in 1864. According to the notes on this water-colour sketch made by the artist Horatio Gordon Robley, the carvings were being prepared for His Excellency the Governor Sir George Grey. From the Robley Collection, Dominion Museum, Wellington.

Specialisation by sub-tribes of the great tribes (for example the *hapu* Ngati Tarawhai and Ngati Whakaue of Te Arawa) produced many experts whose fame spread widely, and calls for whose services came from many distant districts. Thus it is risky to attribute provenience on the basis of style alone. The documentation of carvings in this book is based on written records. Where attribution is based on style this fact is noted.

Nowadays the carving convention best known to New Zealanders and to visitors from overseas is that of the Bay of Plenty and East Coast regions. These two localities maintained a vigorous carving tradition when the carving tradition of other areas, such as Auckland and Taranaki, had expired because of the sudden disruption of Maori life in the early 19th century. The probable causes of survival of carving in some areas was through their relative isolation from the musket wars which ravaged parts of the North Island, and relative isolation from the full impact of European settlement. The East Coast and Bay of Plenty Maori had some time in which to make cultural adjustments, and today these two areas remain strongholds of carving tradition. They have led the way in the revival of carving art, particularly through the inspiration of Sir Apirana Ngata (1874–1950). The establishment of the New Zealand Maori Arts and Crafts Institute by Act of Parliament in 1963, and its practical establishment in 1965 at Whakarewarewa, aided by tourist-trade revenues, from the thermal park, has opened the way for the training of carvers to meet new needs in modern life. It is a challenge calling for the clearest definitions of objectives, for the highest standard of craftsmanship on the part of instructors, and for creative planning on the part of the administrators.

Success in the study of Maori carving will be achieved by relating its aspects to the origins of the Polynesians, the chronology of settlement, basic religious and social ideas, the economics and effect of environment, and tribal styles in the development of the craft. An attempt at systematic arrange-

5⇨ Te Rangihaeata's house "Kai Tangata" as seen by George French Angas about 1844 on the island of Mana near Titahi Bay, Wellington. According to the artist most of the carvings on this house were "executed by Rangihaeata's own hand, and the image supporting the ridge pole is intended to represent himself". From a lithograph in *The New Zealanders Illustrated*, London, 1847.

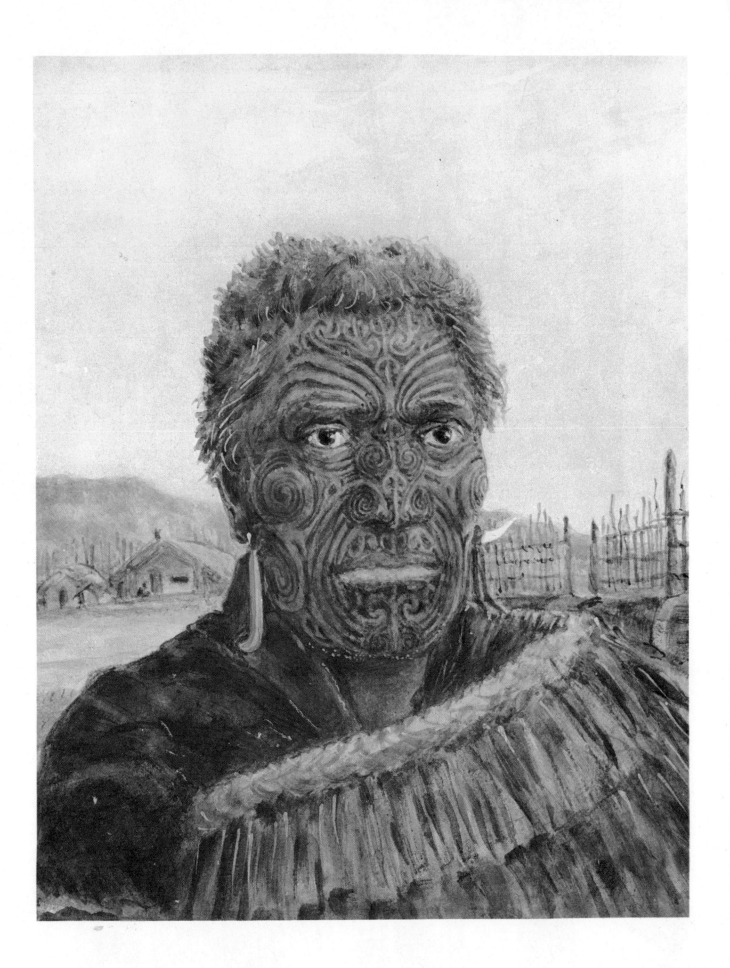

ment of significant factors bearing on the development of Maori carving is found in the table that follows (page 22).

The most important single influence on Maori carving was the concept of mana and tapu, a practical example being the head in sculpture, which was rendered large because it was the most tapu part of the body. The definition of these words is vital to any understanding of Maori culture. The standard definitions and spellings are as in the 6th edition of Herbert W. Williams *A Dictionary of the Maori Language* (revised and augmented under the auspices of the Polynesian Society and published by the Government Printer, Wellington, 1957).

Some Polynesian words are now absorbed into English, notably tattoo (*tatu*), and taboo from the Tongan *tabu* (introduced to Europe as a Polynesian concept by Captain Cook at the end of the 18th century). In Maori, tapu means simply, forbidden, under ceremonial restriction, sacred, and not to be touched. The second word which embodies so much of Polynesian religion is mana, meaning supernatural power, authority, the subtle quality of peoples and things (including the mana of carvings). Mana gives practical effectiveness which can be increased by success or diminished by failure. Contact with anything that pollutes was persistently a danger to the mana of persons or things. The word has connotations in South-East Asia, where it probably relates to Indian *prana*, a kind of psychic force or life essence.

The word tiki, also now in the English vocabulary refers to a human form in wood or other material (e.g., *hei*-tiki .. tiki and *hei*, to suspend). Maori words in the text which have been absorbed well into English are set in ordinary (roman) type, while Maori words still regarded as foreign words by most English speakers are rendered in italic type e.g., *waka-huia, pataka, epa*. Marginal cases such as manaia are here printed in roman type.

The manaia is defined in Williams dictionary as "a grotesque beaked figure often introduced in carving". This strange creature is variously identified or interpreted as a fabulous sea monster (*taniwha*), lizard, bird-man, ghostly spirit, symbol of mana power, or merely a human tiki rendered in profile. It has an important place in this book, and is given further attention below and in many plates that follow.

MANA AND TAPU IN OLD MAORI LIFE

Every aspect of Maori life had, in former days, its own restrictions and ritual requirements. Nowhere were these more important than in the profession of the wood carver. The making and handling of images of ancestors, and the fitting of them into meeting-houses, engendered many taboos and unseen dangers. Food, especially cooked food, was regarded as a potent destroyer of mana, with women running a close second. Both were kept well away from carvers at work and from other vital activities. They were *noa*, that is, common or ordinary, and free from tapu or any other restriction. This was not the difference between good and evil but between positive and negative. The male element was the positively charged, so contact with the female negative could discharge sacred mana. Thus if a cooked kumara or a woman or a pipe (in post-contact times) came near or made contact with carver or carving, loss of mana resulted. For this reason women and food kept away from carvers at work and the smoking of pipes on the job was also tapu until recent times. Nowadays few seem worried by old restrictions.

The mana of a new meeting-house was sometimes contained in a carving transferred from an old house. At the opening of a new house the negative power of a woman's aura was put to use in the tapu-lifting ceremony when a woman or girl of rank merely stepped over the threshold to chant of appropriate *karakia*. This effectively destroyed the residual harmful psychic influences lingering in and around the new house. From the Maori point of view observance of tapu was a deadly serious business. At times human sacrifices were made at the erection of the main posts of a tribal meeting-house of importance. The protection of mana was not a game but a serious matter concerning life and death.

A remarkable incident illustrating the power of belief in mana and tapu especially, in relation to carvers and the building of a house, is found in an account of the erection of Hotonui at Whakatane, in 1878. The story quoted below was told to Gilbert Mair by Mereana Mokomoko, daughter of Apanui Hamaiwaho who built this remarkable house which is now in the Auckland Museum. Mair retold it to the Auckland Institute in 1897 and his talk was printed in the *Transactions of the New Zealand Institute* the following year (see Bibliography).

The building of Hotonui, as with any house of such size, was a major community undertaking which on this occasion involved about seventy

6 ◁ The Ngati Terangi chief Te Kuha of the Bay of Plenty region. Te Kuha was described by artist Horatio Gordon Robley as "a carver in wood of repute" and "the best tattooed man" of his tribe. Robley also notes that Te Kuha had fought against the Pakeha in the Tauranga campaign of 1864. This sketch was made immediately after the battles (for a biographical note on the artist see page 138). From a water-colour in the Robley Collection, Dominion Museum, Wellington.

7 The craft of carving, at least of ritualistic carving art, was believed by the Maori to have originated with the gods. It was a supernatural rather than a mundane craft. Carving practitioners were obliged to avoid the pollution or decline of their mana as they were priests in their own right. According to one traditional belief carving art was introduced to man by Rua. Before then only painted patterns were used. The story is told in the Introduction. The carvings on the façade of Rua's house deceived many, who thought they were living beings. Here a visitor tries to *hongi* with them, much to the amusement of Rua, who knows they are merely images of wood. (*Del.* Dennis Turner)

Ngatiawa from several sub-tribes. All involved worked under the direction of a number of carvers of chiefly rank. All went well until the occurrence of an inadvertent breach of tapu law. Mereana Mokomoko's story gives us an unusually vivid illustration of the strong association of carving and supernatural forces even at this comparatively late period.

The first post erected for Hotonui, commemorating a chief of the Ngati-whanaunga, met difficulty at the erection of the massive ridge beam, which was symbolically the spine of the ancestor. Here are Mereana's words:

When an attempt was made to lift the ridge-pole it failed; then we sent for Paroto Manuta-whiorangi, who uttered an incantation, or karakia, called "Tehuti o Tainui" (the raising of Tainui), and lo! the great tree was lifted up quickly and easily. Such was the power of magic as exercised by Maori priests of old. During the building a number of the Ngatiawa workmen were smitten with sudden illness, which was attributed to their having burned in a cooking-fire some chips from Apanui's chisel (*whao*). It was the women who inadvertently committed sacrilege, and the sickness which fell upon our people was termed a *mate-ruahine*. When several persons had died, my brother Wepiha came to me at dawn of day saying, "*Kua ngaro a Ngatiawa*" (Ngatiawa will be annihilated). Hasten you quickly to remove the spell caused by the desecration of the work of our father's chisel." I hurried to the spot, and in the midst of the assembly a small fire was made of chips from the carvings, and two kumara roasted therein, which were offered to me to eat. I trembled with fear, lest death should come to me also; but the old men said, "Fear not, you are equal in mana to Apanui, your father, and you

alone can remove this spell which is destroying Ngatiawa." I then ate the roasted food, and the epidemic ceased. Soon the house was completed, and Wepiha summoned a *tohunga* called Mohi Taikororeka from Opotiki to perform the ceremonies called "*whai kawa*"—i.e., making the house "*noa*", removing the *tapu* etc. After this was done, and the men had entered and eaten food in the house, three women (myself, Kitemate Kiritahanga, and Mere Taipari) were sent for to *takahi te paepae* (to tread on or cross over the threshold, and thus remove the enchantment which debars women from entering a sacred house until this ceremony is ended), for, as you know, the ridge-pole would sag down in the middle and destroy the appearance of the house were this ceremony disregarded. As the morning star (*Kopu*) rose, we, the three women, crossed over the threshold which Te Raihi, of Ngatihaua, had *tapa'd* (called) Hape Koroki, and then the *mana o te whakairo* (the sacredness of the carving) was subjugated, overcome, and women generally were free to enter and eat within the house.

MATERIALS AND TECHNIQUES

The wood favoured by the Maori carver was the beautiful conifer named by the Maori totara, and by botanists *Podocarpus totara*. It was abundant and grew both on high and low land. Before most of New Zealand's flat-land bush was felled in the 19th century, totara could be found on coasts, lakes, and rivers where it could be easily used in making canoes, houses, and other necessary things.

Totara split readily into long slabs and was relatively soft, two practical qualities appreciated by craftsmen who used stone cutting-tools, wooden wedges and mallets. Also, it was durable despite its tendency to develop surface cracks when exposed to sun and rain.

The largest totaras rose to well over a hundred feet and possessed diameters of up to six or seven feet. A range of intermediate-size trees were available for particular jobs, so required timber was gathered without the expenditure of too much labour. The well seasoned wood of fallen trees was favoured for some tasks, while the whole range of hardwoods and softwoods of the New Zealand bush was exploited for particular uses. For example clubs were made from dense hardwoods selected for the grains and knots suitable for particular weapons. The magnificent kauri pine of the Auckland district was naturally favoured by northern people, as its wood is one of the finest carving materials in the world.

A question often asked by the average museum visitor looking at Maori collections is: "What is the wood?" And the answer is often "I don't know." Some woods, notably totara, are sufficiently distinctive for ready identification, but the grain and colour of wood patinated to brown by long handling, blackened by immersion in swamp mud, or covered by paint, it is not easily seen without scraping the surface and this expedient should never be used. The cracking patterns of totara are clues even when the surface is painted, but this is exceptional.

The modern practice of painting carvings with oilbound paints has not been sufficiently criticised by writers. The old-time Maori covered certain carvings with a variety of red clays mixed with shark liver oil, the mixture being called *kokowai*, but these oxidised iron-bearing clays gave a range of delicate ochreous hues, from red to orange, quite unlike the European red paints now often used on carvings. Also, *kokowai* wore off, leaving rubbed high points and graduated areas which are interesting.

Red, as the sacred colour of the Polynesians, represented the power of the gods and of mana, so the application of red to many carvings had a ritualistic as well as a practical aim. Let us remember that not all carvings were coated *kokowai*, as old carvings in overseas collections eloquently illustrate. In fact, within the 19th century there grew in the minds of New Zealanders, Maori and Pakeha alike, the notion that all respectable Maori carving should be red. Many fine old houses and even those in

museums were painted over to give them a fresh new look. From the point of view of aesthetics it is a sad story. Where houses were exposed to the weather there was a need to paint and to conserve. The error has been in the paints used. Modern paints dry with a hard skin and the red varieties are often of garish hue.

The writer witnessed the distressing sight of an old Rotorua house having its old paint coat, which had weathered over half a century to a soft brownish-red not unlike certain *kokowai* colours, obliterated by a shiny red Dulux enamel. Harsh colour detracts so much from the quality of the carving that a sensitive eye is offended. Criticism of painting over carvings comes from visitors as often as from born New Zealanders. The truth is that many old houses have been covered with new paint when they should have had the old paint preserved. A sad example of this is the house Te Hau-ki-Turanga in the Dominion Museum. Some museums have painted carving simply to enhance displays, but the less thought about this the better.

The colour plates that follow offer many examples of *kokowai*, modern paints, and patinated surfaces. Comment on Maori and European paint is made in a number of captions. Basically Maori art is in the Oceanic tricolour tradition of red, white and black.

A distinctive decorative material of Classic carving which has persisted in modern carving is the use of paua shell (*Haliotis iris*) for circlets, or elliptical pieces of shell inlaid as eyes. These are either fixed on by a central peg or held by pressed fit over a centre boss. These techniques were used also in Hawaii and other Pacific islands. In some North Island areas small paua shells were inlaid complete so as to form the whole eye, but the usual method was to cut the eye forms required from the flat part of fresh paua. Some shells grew as large as six inches in length and always the inner surface reflected light in many colours by its thousands of stria-

⇨ **8** Sir George Grey, Governor of New Zealand through two terms of office (1845–53 and 1861–68), gave distinguished service to Maori and Pakeha alike. He was active in Maori affairs and maintained a deep interest in Maori life and lore. The wood carvings and other artifacts he collected may be seen in several museums, particularly in the collection of the British Museum, London. The incident depicted here seems particularly significant to our understanding of the spirit of the carvers. A group of chiefs failed to appear on time to an appointment they had with Governor Grey, their excuse being that they had been too engrossed with their carving chisels to note the passing of time. However this scene, with gift of a treasure-box as if in conciliation, is purely imaginary. (*Del*. Dennis Turner)

15

tions on the inner surface. The reflected light is of a rich opalescent bluish-green, especially impressive when the flickering of firelight within a house caused the eyes of images to glow and appear to look out at the living.

STONE TOOLS

The kit of stone tools used by Maori carvers was more varied than the kits used elsewhere in Polynesia. The basic types of blades found in New Zealand are readily paralleled elsewhere in Polynesia and even in South-East Asia and on the Asian mainland, but the range of types is unsurpassed. Nephrite (*pounamu*) blades, the so-called "greenstone" adzes, are unique to New Zealand within Polynesia but similar jade implements were used in the Philippine Islands and in ancient China.

Stone adzes and chisels have been classified into types many times over by archaeologists and they are regarded along with fishhooks as a remarkable index to cultural relationships in the Pacific. From the functional point of view not much is known of the actual use of the different stone blades, however, it seems probable that a practical woodworker with a good knowledge of the use of tools could analyse Maori tools in relation to early carvings and thus produce some new technical information. Such a study might well tie up with the changes in carving style with the coming of metal tools, because a change of tools brings change to styles. Unfinished carvings often reveal technical methods where finished carvings do not.

The reluctance of curio gatherers to collect ordinary tools at the time when they were readily available is evident in the absence in collections of complete hafted working adzes of early date. A complete hafted stone adze, now in West Germany, one of the rarest of all Maori artifacts, here makes its first appearance in the literature of the subject. Of the many thousands of stone heads now in collections it is doubtful if a single one has passed direct from the hand of the user to the collector; however, as stone is so durable, surviving surface weathering,

water immersion, or earth burial, this most abundant of all Maori artifacts has survived, though in most instances with visible change.

SURFACE DECORATION

As a general rule Archaic period carvings have little or no surface decoration while the Classic carvings usually have lavish surface decoration, although ornate Classic carving at its best expresses a restrained mood. In the European period, now of two hundred years' duration, surface decoration has steadily assumed a dominant role in Maori wood carving art. Nineteenth-century carvings tend to show extreme lavishness in use of materials, with concentration on surface decoration in opposition to sculptural form, and this tendency became more evident as the 19th century proceeded. The several reasons for change are reviewed in the body of the text, but, simply stated, the cause was the disintegrating influence of western civilisation on Maori culture. The use of metal tools, and the adaptation of European architectural ideas as well as techniques, greatly changed Maori meeting-house structure and size. The history of the decadence of Maori carving is partly a history of increasing preoccupation with surface patterns to the detriment of basic form. Also, the false notion that as things get bigger they get better was widely accepted.

Many early carvings are lavishly decorated with surface patterns of great vigour and beauty but in older work this never dominates form. Many craftsmen of the Classic period, particularly those of the Bay of Plenty-East Coast and Auckland regions, seem to have been compulsively driven to fill in all areas unoccupied by the central symbols with spirals, fragmented manaia, eyes, and abstract decorative patterns. From the time of Captain Cook collectors appreciated highly-decorated carvings so it is possible we gain a biassed impression from extant specimens. Mistaken identification of intricacy with skill and beauty was an unfortunate attitude to carvings which has, to a noticeable degree, helped the preservation of the elaborate carvings rather

9 In old New Zealand there were no papers of apprenticeship or contracts with an employer. When a youth wanted to learn to carve it was comparatively easy if he was of reasonable birth and status. To be born into a sub-tribe or family with a strong carving tradition greatly aided an aspirant in becoming a master craftsman. Learning by doing was a rule, especially through attachment to a master and to his school of carving. Watching, serving, and working on communal projects with teams of carvers made for sound craftsmanship. Respect for the taboos relating to carving art was of course vital to success. Most men could use adze and chisel with more or less skill, but the carving of images required highly trained skill and much personal mana. (*Del.* Dennis Turner)

▷10 The Gisborne chief Raharuhi Rukupo, a leader of the Gisborne or Turanga school of carving of the early 19th century, designed and carved, with the help of eighteen carvers, famous Te Hau-ki-Turanga (pp. 78–83). This great meeting-house now stands in Wellington as the chief treasure of the Dominion Museum. The image inside the door, said to be a self-portrait by the great Raharuhi (102), inspired this artist's vision of how the master may have appeared when carving his own self-image. With mallet and chisel in hand, hair tied in a topknot, and face and thighs well tattooed, Raharuhi Rukupo must have provided a magnificent sight. (*Del.* Vernon King)

than many simpler and often sculpturally better carvings. Surface decoration at its best certainly enhances sculpture but it must not dominate. The inherent beauty of old surface decoration in its diverse forms may be readily studied in many plates. Some of the later carvings depicted in this book illustrate the falling away from the high standard seen in the earlier examples, but a good range of material for each period is illustrated.

No attempt has here been made to analyse surface patterns in detail as variants may be studied directly from the carvings illustrated. To assist the eye a few basic principles may help. In brief, these are the basic patterns: *rauponga*, formed by grooves (*haehae*) and intermediate ridges (*raumoa*) set parallel from one to six, rarely more, which enclose chevron cuts (these are the so-called "dog-tooth notches" (*pakati*)). A zigzag cut or "water pattern", termed *tara-tara-o-kai*, is rare but regularly seen. An uncommon cut, called *unaunahi* or "fish-scales", is formed by half-circle or elliptical ridges set within grooves or spirals. A variant of *unaunahi* is the *pakura*, so named because of its resemblance to the foot impression left by the swamp hen when walking over soft ground. Some patterns occur regularly on certain artifacts, for example the *tara-tara-o-kai* is typically found on storehouse carvings.

Surface decoration is immensely varied and its analysis could well be given monographic study by some patient investigator. Whether surface patterns possessed any mystic symbolism or whether they evolved from forms or as mere decorative embellishment has yet to be revealed. At this stage little is known on the subject. One bulb-like motif termed *koru* is said to have been inspired by the young fern frond and is also used as a primary unit in many painted rafter designs (*kowhaiwhai*). *Koru* is conventionally regarded as having little association with carved patterns, yet it is found on several wood carvings of early date and it has been favoured, frequently with bad results, by late 19th and 20th century carvers.

THE SPIRAL

The spiral is the most distinctive surface decoration of Classic Maori carving of the North Island—particularly that of the Bay of Plenty-East Coast and Auckland districts. It is in fact one of the most distinctive artistic motifs found in New Zealand although its complexity and lavish use are rivalled in other parts of Oceania. In Pacific art it has ancient forebears, notably in South-East Asia and ancient China. The diffusion of the spiral with development in local areas seems a more acceptable theory of its origin than the popular notion of local development.

The Maori use of spirals, whether simple or complex, is closely paralleled in Borneo and New Guinea. Within Polynesia the Marquesas Islands offer the closest parallel to the spiral of Classic carving, but in the Marquesas the spirals tended to be rendered in rectilinear, "fretted" forms.

When spirals appear on an image they tend to radiate from a centre of movement, such as the shoulders, elbows, buttocks, knees, ankles, tongue, and corners of the mouth. In suggesting that spirals often serve as points of movement or joint marks, it is important to note that faces occasionally appear on the body and these presumably had magical significance in early imagery. Carl Schuster, in a paper entitled *Joint Marks: a possible index of cultural contact between America, Oceania and the Far East*, includes New Zealand as an important Pacific area in this particular study of the dispersal of a theme.

Manaia heads commonly appear superimposed on ancestral images, and stray eyes occur sporadically in a way that suggests that they are vestiges of manaia heads, or that they represent manaia. If bird-human relationships in Melanesia are compared with manaia-tiki relationships in Maori carving, the parallels are striking. Sometimes simple interlocking spirals are formed in Maori carving by the inter-

11 Maori carvers were inspired and guided by the old Polynesian religion that their distant ancestors had carried from tropical Polynesia. Its basic beliefs, social concepts and domestic controls remained more or less stable, yet adapted to New Zealand conditions. To the old-time Polynesians all things possessed a spirit and mana of their own and were under the tutelage of a particular god. For this reason rituals were required before any natural or man-made thing could be touched or used, for example even a common adze had its personal spirit and was thus chanted over before work. Here a group of chiefly carvers are seen in an act of placating Tane, Lord of Forests, before felling a giant totara with their stone adzes. The sprigs of green leaves they hold had an important function in many tapu lifting ceremonies. (Del. Vernon King)

locking jaws or "beaks" of manaia, a device that is used in Northern Melanesia where bird beaks are interlocked to make fairly complex surface patterns.

SYMBOLISM

The range of symbols found in Maori Classic carving is seen to be restricted when it is compared with several other Pacific cultures. In most Oceanic arts there are two basic symbols: one is the human form representing ancestor or god, with variations such as hybrid bird-men; the other is the bird. Classic Maori carving has as its central symbol the human image or tiki which commonly represents an ancestor and, on very rare occasions, a god or human portrait; while the second major symbol is a beaked creature called manaia. The implications are self-evident.

Secondary or minor motives are: a sea monster or merman called *marakihau*, the whale (*pakake*) which may represent a *taniwha* (water monster), and the lizard (*moko*). The dog (*kuri*) appears once or twice. Each of these symbols is later considered in detail in relation to the illustrations. Here a few general comments preface the discussion of actual specimens. It is particularly important to state that the bases of several interpretations made in this book are not conventionally acceptable to all ethnologists who have written on Maori carving.

Ancestral images are commonly placed in the stance of war dance with contorted limbs and bulging eyes as may be seen on house panels and posts. Some ancestors are depicted with club in hand and tongue out-thrust in defiance, features accentuating the warlike posture. The head, being the most significant part of the body in Maori belief, had intensive mana centred on it, and for this reason it is made so large that it is out of proportion to the body. This treatment of the head also helped in fitting the human form to posts and panels to meet architectural requirements which in turn influenced sculpture in many ways. For example the head is often flattened to fill the upper part of a panel while the brows are drawn out into peaks to fill upper corners.

The out-thrust tongue is not only an expression of defiance but also of magic. It provided at least some protection from evil forces. The erect penis of many images symbolises both the virility of the ancestor and, with the out-thrust tongue, protective power. This symbolism has ancient antecedents in Pacific arts where exposure of tongue or penis is regarded as an aggressive as well as a protective act.

SEXUAL SYMBOLISM

Throughout the world one finds unmistakable sexual symbols in traditional sculpture and nowhere is this more so than in the Pacific. The 19th century Victorian tradition has conditioned many to a one-eyed view in matters of sex but generations following World War II find it easy to accept sexual symbols. One suspects that generations of New Zealanders regarded Maori carving as somewhat gross, if not obscene, and avoided studying it too closely. The author has seen notes on a manuscript asking the blockmaker to remove the sexual organs from the printed version. Dozens of carvings have been emasculated because they offended puritanical owners, while many perfectly innocent ancestral figures have been wrapped round with skirts in meeting-houses and in museum galleries.

Let us look at the facts. The Pacific practice of using enlarged sexual organs and depicting human copulation in carving is symbolical and in no way pornographic or aimed at stimulating erotic pleasure. The phallic elements in Maori carving, which are so persistent and obvious, are expressive of the desire for tribal survival, virility in war, and protection from the malignant forces of the unseen world.

There is no evidence of phallic worship of a Maori Priapus. It is true that the penis, vulva and coitus were treated in a more earthy way than in tropical Polynesia, and one can attribute this only to the intensive secularisation of Maori religion and life as compared for example with that of the Tahitian and Hawaiian societies. Also, the aim of the tropical image makers was to represent the gods, but in New Zealand most of the carver's attention was directed to portraying tribal ancestors, whose generative function was so highly regarded. These flesh-and-blood ancestors of the man carving the image were not so greatly distant in his genealogy. In fact, the Maori gave little attention to carving wooden images of his gods. The secularisation of the Maori relates to the settlement of Polynesian sea migrants who found at last a group of large islands possessing abundant raw materials. The lack of firm limits to population expansion, and the stimulation of a temperate climate which encouraged independence, and the development of tribes and sub-tribes with territorial rights and demands, gave rise to aggressive warfare.

While the sexual organs of man possessed positive power, the sexual organs of women possessed a negative power believed capable of destroying mana and of frustrating supernatural forces. Women of rank were called on to lift tapu from a house or other object by the negative power of their sex. The door lintels (pare) often have on them one or more female figures, the most notable being those of Taranaki, whose figures draw back the thighs to expose the vulva. The reason is simple—any person entering or leaving a house thus passed beneath the female vulva which, although merely of wood, possessed power to discharge any harmful psychic forces clinging to those who passed beneath. Prudery in the judgment of such carvings by the standards of another culture is unfair, to say the least.

Small figures emerging from the vagina or set between the legs appear to represent birth and to symbolise tribal continuity. Some carvings may represent Maui being strangled to death in the vagina of Hine-nui-te-Po, goddess of death; a late panel in Hamburg certainly does bear this interpretation, but the general theory is unproven.

THE THREE-FINGERED HAND

The so-called "three fingered hand" found on many ancestral figures is commonly composed of three fingers and a back-bending thumb or spur—in other words there are four fingers. There are many quaint myths and stories rationalising this feature but the best interpretation emerges from a comparative study of a wide range of Pacific image material. This reveals that the superimposition of avian features on the human images is widespread, and that this process takes place in New Zealand sculpture as may be seen in the plates that follow. The elliptically shaped and staring eyes and claw-like three-fingered hands confirm the hybrid nature of much Maori scuplture.

An avian theory to help analyse tiki and manaia has been postulated by this author on a number of occasions, and most recently in relation to material representatives of the bird-man in Polynesia (Barrow, 1967). However this general theory was stated in 1959 in a footnote to the paper on free-standing Maori images (see Bibliography), and is here reproduced:

I believe that avian elements are superimposed on the basically human image. The claw hand, slanting eyes, elongated lips and webbed feet (in northern carving) may be thus interpreted. When hybridisation is advanced we secure forms which are termed "bird-men". Indeed the combination of avian and human elements is a regular feature in Oceanic art, reaching out of Indonesia, through Melanesia and into Polynesia where the symbol has a marginal distribution: i.e., New Zealand,

⇨ **12** The art of adzing was regarded as the primary skill of the Maori carver and the adze his most important tool. Adzes ranged from those with blades of a few ounces in weight to massive two handed types with stone heads of ten or more pounds. The Polynesian life of old New Zealand functioned well without benefit of metal or machines as there was no pressure from time clocks or money profit. Craftsmen had time to work in a leisurely way but with full vigour. Here we see a carver swinging a hafted adze with rhythmical and forceful stroke. All massive wood-working began with a large adze dressing, then smaller adzes and chisels finished the blocking-out stage. Surface patterns created by skilful adzing were much esteemed by tribal critics. (Del. Dennis Turner)

Chatham Islands, Easter Island, the Marquesas, and Hawaii. Avian elements appear to be closely associated with the supernatural, or rather, appear as symbols of it. The important symbol in Maori carving termed the *manaia* I believe is basically avian in origin, assuming human characters in many of its forms, and producing "bird-men" of distinctive type. The association of *manaia* with the human image, its aggressive and apparently malignant behaviour, biting and grasping at the ancestor, suggest that it is a kind of demon or spirit, probably of the *atua ngau tangata* or "man-biting god" class.

The suggestion that manaia represent a particular class of inferior god is proposed as a suggestion only. Over the intervening years the writer has moved more to the view that the manaia is a carrier of the mana of the ancestral image it accompanies, but this again is only speculation. It is only with regard to the physical characteristics of manaia that one can make positive statements as its form may be analysed by conjurative study. Regarding this question of manaia representing mana, the author quite casually over a dinner-table asked his friend Dr Mary Kuwena Pukui, co-author of the University of Hawaii *Hawaiian Dictionary*, "Does the word manaia have any meaning in Hawaiian?" Her reply was, "Yes—it means containing mana!" Dr Pukui had not regarded my question as other than a simple one of Polynesian linguistics, and there was no thought of the New Zealand carving symbol in her mind.

The manaia symbol is given liberal space in the text, and is commented on in many places. It is second only to the tiki in order of importance—at least in typical Classic Bay of Plenty-East Coast carving. A claim that its identity is explained by simply accenting it as a human form rendered in profile is not tenable. The notable exponent of the latter view, Sir Gilbert Archey, has received support of the interpretation from Sir Peter Buck and Mr J. M. McEwen (see Bibliography). It is true that when two manaia are brought together they form a kind of face, a device which has been used in with manaia-like animals in the art of ancient China, Borneo, Solomon Islands, British Columbia, and elsewhere in the Pacific. However, in New Zealand as elsewhere, when fabulous profile creatures are joined face to face the resulting face is a mask basically supra-human in character. In areas where this artistic device is used one sees hybridisation of elements, such as birds, dogs, and crocodiles.

There is in fact a distinct profile form of the tiki, termed in Arawa carving tradition *ngutu*. This is quite unlike the manaia although it is often confused with it. A vertical division down the centreline of many tiki heads makes two *ngutu*, and in this respect half a face can yield profiles of a type, but not necessarily manaia.

The point that must be stressed is that European logical interpretations cannot be superimposed on any traditional art, and least of all on a stone-age art such as that of the Maori. Primitive arts have their roots in mystical religious ideas and unusual social customs which are remote from modern scientific thought. This book presents the fruits of systematic searching and collecting, but the analyses offered are in the traditions of an ethnographical method and of art history established in the 19th century which, at best, are wisely left flexible—they are in a sense "open-ended". This is the author's attitude to the problem of manaia and tiki, and indeed to the other symbols of Maori carving.

Augustus Hamilton in *Maori Art* refers to manaia as a "mythological animal . . . probably a kind of *taniwha*". The *taniwha* is a reptilian water monster formerly much feared by the Maori. The supernatural association of manaia seems likely, but its display of both human and avian features when in its characteristic types, is obvious. However some insist on the theory of exclusive human derivation and reject the self-evident. The reader is asked to observe the many manaia and to try to make up his own mind on the question.

Briefly reviewed, the author's opinion is that manaia is of highly complex physical form composed of human and bird elements intermixed, with occasional additional animal features derived from reptiles and sea creatures admixed. To Pacific man, birds and reptiles were very much of a kind, as they are zoologically. The lizard (*moko*), so important in Maori belief, probably influenced manaia.

The folk memory of the crocodile of Melanesia is reasonably established by Skinner and reinforces this relationship.

The use of birds, bird-man variants, or the addition of bird features to ancestral images, is widespread in the Pacific arts. This sculptural tradition originates in the firm association of birds with the souls of the dead and with spirits in general. Birds acted as spirit vehicles. In Maori belief certain bird species, such as the owl (*ruru*), were favoured as personal or tribal totems, omen-carriers, and guardians. Maori myths relate certain carvings to owls, notably in their personified form of Koururu. Here is a significant quotation from Elsdon Best:

East coast myths attribute carvings to one Rua-i-te-pukenga, who introduced the art into this world, having acquired it in the realm of Rangi-tamaku, the second of the twelve heavens, counting upward. Rongo also acquired his knowledge of carving and carved designs from the house of Warekura in that celestial realm. When he constructed his own house he used Koururu (personified form of owl) as a sacred offering, and buried his body under the rear wall of the house. The Maori tells us that this is the reason why carved figures have large glaring eyes; they are the eyes of Koururu.

The carvings that follow aim at enabling a review to be made of the manaia, tiki, and of other Maori symbols in relation to actual material. They are more important than interpretations. As for the word manaia, it is possible that this is not the original term applied to the carving motif. Manaia does not appear in early editions of William's *Dictionary*. However it is believed that this word is proto-Polynesian and probably two or three thousand years old. It occurs in several islands with related meanings, such as "a chief", "beautiful decoration", a certain lizard, and the seahorse.

Augustus Earle as early as 1832 made a tantalising reference to what might be construed as manaia. He says: "One of their favourite subjects [in carving] is a lizard taking hold of a man's head: their tradition being that this was the origin of man." Augustus Hamilton in his several suggestions regarding manaia says it "may have been considered as representations of lizard". In 1916 Elsdon Best noted that: "The Maori has a dim idea that the origin of the manaia design was some denizen of the ocean", but in *The Maori*, 1924, he cautioned that "in the face of several unreliable statements that have been published concerning this peculiar design, it is well to record the fact that the Maori has no real knowledge of its origin."

Today we can only speculate and look at actual material. The reptilian monsters, called *naga*, which are marine creatures, part reptile and part bird, and which are seen regularly in the art of India and Indonesia, should not be left out of our consideration. The *naga* in some of its forms closely resembles manaia. Similar dragon-like creatures seen on the bronzes of Shang and Chou China, made a thousand years before Christ, also offer striking parallels to manaia.

The postulation of a probable relationship between the art motifs of Polynesia and ancient China is supported by scholars who have made comparative studies. These theories were reviewed in the book (1966) entitled *Two Studies of Art in the Pacific Areas* comprising studies by Robert Heine Geldern (*A note on the relations between the art styles of the Maori and Ancient China*) and Mino Badner (*The protruding tongue and related motifs in the art styles of the American Northwest Coast, New Zealand and China*) (see Bibliography).

ORIGINS OF CARVING ART

Pioneer efforts will lead to thorough monographic studies in future decades. These studies of the future can expect better support from archaeological and cultural data than is at present available. The origin and development of Maori carving has been the subject of debate over a number of decades and many contributions are bypaths. Regarding the origins of wood sculpture there are two schools of thought: one claims that the main features of Maori carving evolved in New Zealand, while the other claims that the basic elements were imported from afar. Both schools are right if rightly interpreted.

It is well known that the Polynesian peoples inhabited the islands within a vast triangle with Hawaii at its apex, Easter Island in the extreme south-east, and New Zealand in the south-western corner over a time span of less than three thousand years. All things considered Polynesian culture is relatively homogeneous because of its derivation from related traditions and subsequent isolation.

The ancestors of the Maori brought working tools, techniques, and artistic themes with them. When they reached New Zealand they found abundant supplies of good wood, and rocks ideal for stone tools—two essentials to the development of a notable wood art in a stone age culture. All things considered, Maori art has a sophisticated quality that suggests relationship with ancient civilisations. In the circumstances it can best be understood by regarding it as the development, in a favourable environment, of ancient themes and traditions derived in the immediate past from eastern Polynesia. From there we must look westwards to the margins of Melanesia, to South-East Asia, and thence to the Asian mainland.

The movement of the peoples who became Polynesians is being worked out in terms of basic economy including the study of plants and animals and the study of primary artifacts such as adzes and fishhooks. The study of art motifs in isolation is too subjective. However, the rapid progress of Pacific archaeology over the last two decades with its analysis of the dispersal of man over the Pacific over time and space will in due course provide answers to the question of Maori origins. At this time it seems reasonable to relate Classic Maori carving to that of the Marquesas Islands, at least that is where we see the closest visual relationship within Polynesia. Archaeological evidence may support the theory of direct migrations from the Marquesas to New Zealand about the 14th century, but we cannot as yet be certain of this. Archaic or Moa-Hunter origins and arts of the early period are seen to relate more directly to the Society and Cook Islands but this general observation is as much as we are entitled to make.

There are several traditional stories telling of the origin of carving art among men. The most well known thanks Rua, who is said to have taken carvings from the great sea god Tangaroa to his home on shore and copied them for his own house. A convenient source of reference to the stories of Rua and related tales is the extensive collection of myths and legends patiently collected by A. W. Reed under the title *Treasury of Maori Folklore*.

Rua, it appears, was a remote ancestor not quite in the god class but capable of performing supernatural acts. Although living in the world, he could interfere with the gods themselves as did the great Maui before him. Here is the essential story.

The son of Rua when sailing his small canoe was captured by the sea-god Tangaroa and taken to his sea-floor house where he was placed at the gable peak as a *tekoteko*—that is, as a pinnacle image. Frantically searching for his son, Rua swam down to Tangaroa's house, which he entered after coming to friendly terms with the old doorkeeper, Hinematikotai. Once inside he found carved images talking to each other. Later, with the connivance of

* CHART OF TABULATED INFORMATION ON THE MAORI CARVER IN RELATION

It is important to remember that each period overlapped those which preceded and followed, and that changes came gradually.

Periods or phases of Maori culture	Type of Society prevalent, and modifying influences	Status of carver and attitude of society	Value of the carver to the community and symbols used
FIRST PERIOD Archaic Maori or Moa-Hunter 9th century to AD 1350. The latter date is used here for convenience, but the existence of a single fleet is in doubt. This period not seen by Europeans.	Settlers of Eastern Polynesian origin adapting their tropical culture to a temperate climate and to new resources. All evidence is from archaeological excavations and comparative study of related Polynesian cultures.	Little is known of this period but there is good reason to assume status of carver was that of craftsman-priest.	Producer of goods necessary for domestic and ceremonial life. Symbols little known but human image a common motif.
SECOND PERIOD Classic Maori or Fleet Maori A.D. 1350 to A.D. 1769. The latter is the year of Captain James Cook's landing on the shores of New Zealand. This period not seen by Europeans.	Development of distinctly New Zealand variant of Eastern Polynesian culture. Full utilisation of local resources of wood, bone, and stone. The flowering period of Maori culture.	Intense interest of the community with well-informed criticism of quality of work. Highly favourable circumstances for good work. Status of craftsman-priest continued.	Producer of goods essential in warfare, domestic, ceremonial, and religious life. Production of carvings which contribute to prestige of tribe. Manufacture of human images commemorating ancestors.
THIRD PERIOD European contact period A.D. 1769 to A.D. 1869. This period ranges from the arrival of Captain Cook to the period of full-scale settlement by Europeans. Abundant observations of Maori culture.	Steady decline of traditional values. Influence of European modes of living. Christianity replaces the Maori religious system.	Decline of status to that of honoured craftsman. Overtone of religious power and special rights steadily declines. Slackening of social interest.	Preoccupation with European goods lessens importance of carver's service to community. Decline and extinction of some forms, and in some areas complete extinction of traditional wood carving. Ceremonial house remains important. New and non-traditional ideas introduced.
FOURTH PERIOD Modern period A.D. 1869 to the present. Period of greatest disintegration of traditional Maori culture, with progressive integration of the Maori people with Pakeha society.	Transformation of Maori society. Traditional values affecting the crafts virtually extinct. Abandonment of many artistic forms.	Further decline in status of carver to that of skilled worker. Complete loss of priestly status. Little public knowledge or informed criticism.	Most carved items once necessary to Maori life no longer required. Meeting-house greatly modified until it approximates European hall in style. Production of tourist curios.

*Adapted from *The Life and Work of the Maori Carver*, T. Barrow, Wellington, 1963.

the doorkeeper, Rua hid himself outside until Tangaroa entered the house with his retinue of attendants to sleep for the night. Then, Rua quietly sealed up all the cracks which would reveal the coming of day. The sun was greatly abhorred by Tangaroa and his folk, and nothing disconcerted them more than rays of sunlight. When the morning sun arose Rua "set fire to the house"—that is, unsealed the cracks—then waited at the door to strike all who ventured out into the blinding light. Some were killed and some escaped, but we are not told how Tangaroa fared. The interesting point of the story is that Rua gathered some of the carvings before they were burnt, and that the ones he selected were those that could not talk. Had Rua taken those with the power of speech, the legend says, "the posts of houses would still have the ability to talk".

When Rua returned to the world with his rescued son he brought with him the carvings, which were the models for his later work and for the men who learnt this wood carving art over the generations that followed. Before Rua's time there were only painted patterns seen on the houses of living men. Thus an old proverb preserves the achievement of Rua in these words: *Nga mahi whakairo, nga mahi a Rua*. The art of carving is the art of Rua.

TO THE PERIODS OF MAORI CULTURE, MAORI SOCIETY, MATERIALS, AND TOOLS.

This chart gives general trends and is designed to aid more advanced study of the life and work of the Maori carver.

Religious sanctions and power of tapu	Attitude to tools and raw materials	Method of payment to carvers attitude to work	Carving style of the period
Craftsman works under influence of Polynesian religious beliefs. Power of *tapu* and ceremonial vital to craft activity.	Polished stone tools. Reverential attitude to both tools and materials.	Eastern Polynesian custom of payment by food and goods. Work of the carver virtually work of the gods.	Carvings few and fragmentary. Simple sculptural style closely allied to that of tropical Polynesia.
Continued background of old Polynesian belief in power of gods, ancestral spirits, and supernatural forces, all of which have influence on affairs of men. Tapu intense, with rituals before undertaking craft activity.	Polished stone tools including nephrite (greenstone/jade) manufactured by the craftsman. Ceremonies over tools to render them more effective. Timber acquired with much labour and after appropriate rituals to Tane (god of the forest).	Payment by food and goods. Time in work not considered or calculated. Prestige accruing to tribe important. No sense of Maori art as a national art. Little sense of individuality in work.	Great variety of carved objects. Restrained style with abundant surface decoration which remains subordinate to sculptural form. Surface decoration soft and comparatively shallow.
Decline of traditional religious beliefs through general breakdown of traditional Maori life and the influence of Christianity.	Stone tools rapidly replaced by improvised chisels and adzes made from whatever iron or copper available. Finally, introduction of forged European-style adzes, chisels, and other tools. Decline in rituals over tools and in obtaining timber. Steady increase in use of pit-sawn timber.	Traditional gift payment continues but European goods and money included. Growing sense of time factor in work and place of individual craftsman. National feeling for Maori art as a means of reviving Maori culture.	Wide changes of style through the influence of European ideas. The new iron and steel tools lessen old restraint, with growth of over-elaboration of surface. Surface decoration deeply cut and high sharp ridges become increasingly evident. Less importance given to sculptural form.
Christian basis of Maori society established and with it the extinction of Maori religion. Traditional tapu system lifted.	Full kit of European carpenters' tools employed. Loss of the old reverence for tools, and omission of traditional rituals. Machine-cut wood purchased from sawmill or timber merchant.	Until about 1940 carving still a potent force in keeping alive traditional Maori values. Decline after World War II. Work by agreed contract for money on an estimated time basis. Individual craftsman emerges.	Further elaboration but declining discipline. Non-traditional methods and motifs introduced. Sharp tempered chisels leave clean high ridges in surface decoration. Much copying and little creative imagination after late 19th century.

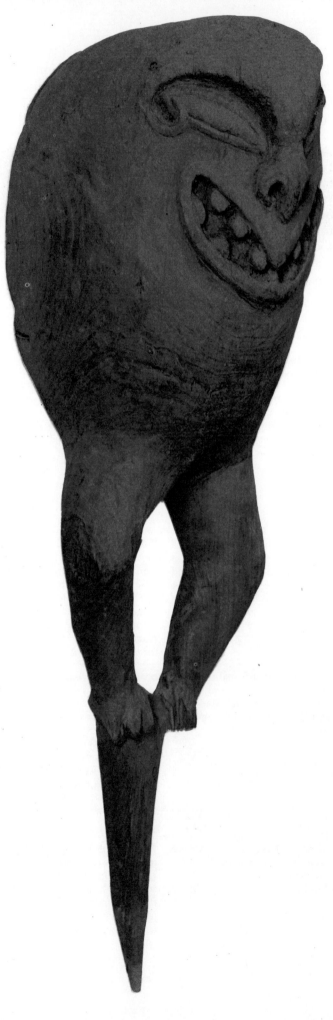

CERTAIN WOODCARVINGS are regarded as being of Archaic style regardless of actual age. This curious small image which has a hollow inside and a door at the back was made to hold a human skull. From a cave at Whangaroa, North Auckland. *Height:* 26″ (66cm). *Collection:* Auckland Institute and Museum, Auckland.

In old New Zealand the skull of an important chief was treated with special care when his bones were disinterred two or three years after the first burial, in a ceremony known as *hahunga*. In death, as in life, the head was the most tapu part of the body. This specimen represents one distinctive northern Maori carving style known from a few extant carvings (for example, 21). Its general manner and special features relate it to Hawaiian carvings which share a common ancestor in the tropical islands of Eastern Polynesia (for other bone-chests see 47–48, 62–63, 129–133).

13 ⇩ From a cave at Whangaroa, North Auckland. *Height* 26″ (66cm). *Collection* Auckland Institute and Museum, Auckland.

14 ⏁

The famous "Kaitaia carving" from a drainage channel cut in a swamp at Kaitaia, Northland. *Width:* 7'5″ (226cm). *Height:* 1'11″ 33cm). *Collection:* Auckland Institute and Museum, Auckland.

This carving is without doubt the most controversial in the literature of Maori art. There are two schools of thought on its identification: one says it is a house door-lintel, while the other claims that it is a roof carving from a raised mortuary house.

Dr H. D. Skinner, in 1964 (see Bibliography) stated a good case for his ridge carving theory, namely: that the carving was finished on both sides and thus contrasted with door lintels, which are left unfinished behind; that the base is hollow and formed in a manner which suggests that it was cut to fit a ridge; and that the positions of the lashing holes are consistent with ridge fastening.

The style of the carving is closely paralleled by certain carvings of Raivavae in the Austral Islands. As the style of the carving is Polynesian, the Kaitaia carving may not be presented as evidence of a pre-Polynesian people in New Zealand although association of it with mythical pre-Maori settlers was common for some time after its discovery. The identification of the outward-turned creatures at either end remains a mystery, yet it is not unreasonable to relate them to the manaia of Classic carving (see pages 62–67).

15 ⇩
Canoe prow (*tau-ihu*) found in a partly drained swamp behind sand dunes at the northern end of Doubtless Bay in North Auckland. *Length:* 42″ (104cm). *Collection:* Auckland Institute and Museum, Auckland.

The style of this prow is closely related to the Awanui slab (16) and is in addition associated with a sternpost of a similar style from Doubtless Bay in the collection of the Auckland Museum. Such carvings as this one seems remote from carvings of the familiar "Classic" style yet there are basic similarities. This prow has the primary and secondary heads found on fishing-canoe prows of the Historic period, although in Classic convention the secondary head is a manaia rendered behind the primary mask. These heads are evidently humanised bird heads and are more than stylised human heads (see pages 56–58).

16 ⇩
Wooden panel with birdlike figures. From Awanui, Northland. *Length:* 5′5″ (165cm). *Width:* 1′2″ (35.5cm). *Collection:* Auckland Institute and Museum, Auckland.

This carved board, from a house or store structure falls into the pre-Classic carving group. It was discovered fortuitously during swamp drainage operations at Awanui. The heads and images carved on it have strange points which probably represent feathers. In style it is related to the Doubtless Bay canoe prow (15) which has similar projecting spikes or points which also suggest feathers. The heads at the end of the board provide evidence for the type of head which formerly existed on the now decapitated standing figures. The images of this slab are removed in space and time from the Nuku-te-Apiapi door panel (49), yet their inspiration arises from similar ideas.

⇧
17–18 ⇩
Amulet in form of a dog. *Length:* 3″ (7.5cm). *Collection:*
Canterbury Museum, Christchurch.

This unique small carving was found in Monck's Cave,
Sumner, near Christchurch. Its exact purpose is not known
but the suspension hole formed by the curled tail suggests it
was worn as an amulet. Some of the earliest settlers of New
Zealand from Eastern Polynesia successfully introduced the
Asian domestic dog but it makes an appearance in carving
art on only one or two occasions. The style of this dog is
reminiscent of the *haniwa* sculptures of Japan. It entirely
lacks surface decoration. The earliest carvers of New Zealand
were more concerned with form than the surface elaboration
which became such a distinctive feature of Classic sculpture
and which led to the unrestrained surface decorations of
much 19th and 20th century work.

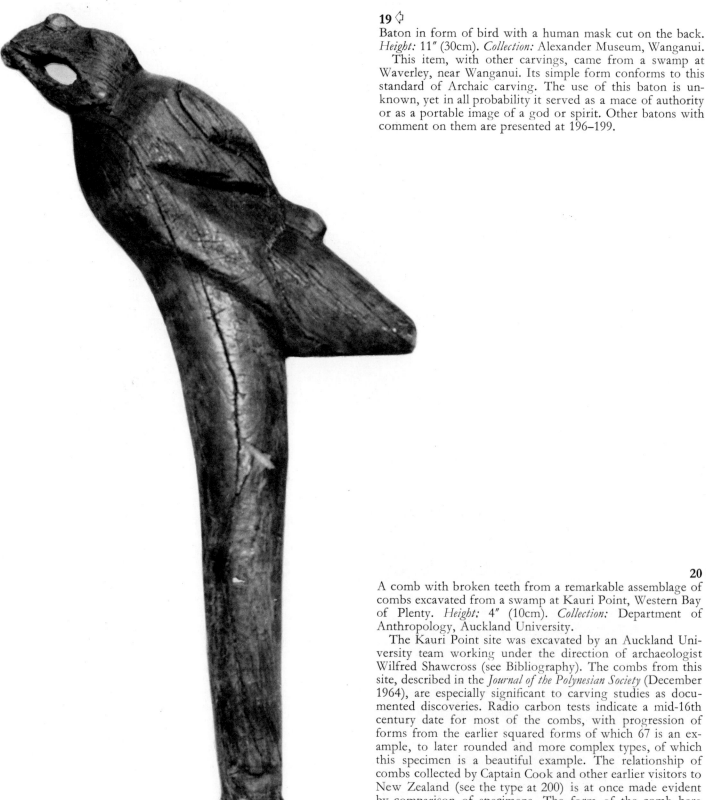

19 ⇦
Baton in form of bird with a human mask cut on the back. *Height:* 11″ (30cm). *Collection:* Alexander Museum, Wanganui.

This item, with other carvings, came from a swamp at Waverley, near Wanganui. Its simple form conforms to this standard of Archaic carving. The use of this baton is unknown, yet in all probability it served as a mace of authority or as a portable image of a god or spirit. Other batons with comment on them are presented at 196–199.

20 ⇨
A comb with broken teeth from a remarkable assemblage of combs excavated from a swamp at Kauri Point, Western Bay of Plenty. *Height:* 4″ (10cm). *Collection:* Department of Anthropology, Auckland University.

The Kauri Point site was excavated by an Auckland University team working under the direction of archaeologist Wilfred Shawcross (see Bibliography). The combs from this site, described in the *Journal of the Polynesian Society* (December 1964), are especially significant to carving studies as documented discoveries. Radio carbon tests indicate a mid-16th century date for most of the combs, with progression of forms from the earlier squared forms of which 67 is an example, to later rounded and more complex types, of which this specimen is a beautiful example. The relationship of combs collected by Captain Cook and other earlier visitors to New Zealand (see the type at 200) is at once made evident by comparison of specimens. The form of the comb here illustrated provides a clue that the form of most Classic combs collected in historic times is originally based on the human head with the nose feature rendered as a manaia. For another Kauri Point comb see 67.

21 ⇦

Wooden short club (*patu-rakau*), from a swamp at Ohaewai, Northland. *Dimensions:* 10¼″ (26cm) × 7⅛″ (8cm) × 1⅜″ (3.5cm). K. A. Webster *Collection*.

The rare style of treatment of the head, namely of mouth, teeth, eyes and nose, compares closely with the face of the Kauri Point comb (2) and Whangaroa skull box (13). One side of the club (which might also qualify as a baton of the type defined on pages 142–143), is virtually uncarved while the other side, here illustrated, is covered with surface decoration composed of the *pitau* (circinate frond of fern) or *koru* element. This design element is rarely found in wood carving yet often used for painted rafter patterns (*kowhaiwhai*) or for incised patterns on gourds (*hue*).

⇨ **22**

A short club (*patu*) from Horowhenua, Wellington. *Height:* 16¼″ (41.2cm). *Collection:* Dominion Museum.

In 1963 a Wellington Technical College boy named David Baoumgren came to the author's office at the Dominion Museum with this carving wrapped in a piece of brown paper. David had been out rabbiting near Levin and while on the beach near the mouth of the Hokio Stream, which flows out of Lake Horowhenua, he found this *patu* lying on the sand. He thought it might have drifted from Easter Island, which was a clever association of *patu* with the carving style of Easter Island, but its wood is heavier than water; also, distance, tide, and sea current ruined such a theory. It is probable this *patu* was washed out of the bed of Lake Horowhenua then pushed down the bottom of the Hokio Stream to be thrown on to the beach by a seawave along with the thousands of pieces of driftwood to be seen along the Otaki beaches after a storm. ●

23 ⬦
Male image with broken arms and legs. *Height:* 8¼″ (21cm).
Collection: Otago Museum, Dunedin.

   This carving, one of the very few to come out of the South
Island, was found in a cave on Okia Flat, Wickliffe Bay,
Otago Peninsula. It is usually regarded as representing a god
rather than an ancestor, as its form resembles certain stick-
gods of the Maori (see pages 104–107). It was published by
the author as a godstick, but without adequate evidence (see
Bibliography, Barrow 1961). The form of this image is
austere, highly conventionalised, and completely lacking
surface decoration. Stylistically it is related to the dog from
Monck's Cave (17–18) and may well represent, along with
the dog, a widespread South Island woodcarving tradition
which is virtually unknown to us through lack of specimens.
Thousands of adzeheads found in South Island sites attest to
the former existence of an extensive wood sculpture in the
South Island.

24-25 ↺ ↻
Godstick (*tiki wananga*). *Height:* 13″ (33cm). *Collection:* Otago Museum, Dunedin.

This godstick is the only recorded specimen from the South Island. The two heads are joined back to back in the manner of the Classic period specimen (138–139), and their stylisation is closely related to that of the double headed images of Easter Island. The shaft is lenticular and thus in contrast to North Island godsticks, which are typically round in cross-section. If this godstick was collected completely with shaft binding, the latter has been unravelled and lost. Dr H. D. Skinner acquired this godstick for the Otago Museum after it had been used as a window prop for some years, thus saving for posterity one of the rarest treasures of Maori craftmanship.

33

I N CLASSIC MAORI CARVING the head is usually rendered as very large in proportion to the body on which it is set. A good example of this relationship of head and body is seen in the personal portrait of Raharuhi Rukupo (102) and in the low relief panel from Te Hau-ki-Turanga illustrated as the frontispiece. The practice of making the head much larger than the body stressed its symbolical importance, and met the carver's need to widen and flatten the head to fill the upper area of the available carving surface. Thus aesthetic and architectural as well as religious requirements were well served.

Both religious and design ideas, as expressed in carving, determined to a great degree the basic image conventions of Maori wood sculpture. The custom of wearing deep facial tattoo (*moko*) had a strong influence on the surface designs of Maori wood-carving in the Classic period as may be readily seen in the more naturalistic portraits (31, 32).

The relationship of facial tattoo of the individual man is also important as personal tattoo patterns were often better remembered than individual facial features. In Maori custom human heads were kept in lifelike preservation by a steaming, smoking and oiling. The mummified heads of one's own tribe or sub-tribe were kept for reasons of affection, while those of enemies were chiefly valued as objects to be insulted and humiliated. The powerful expression seen in the heads of living chiefs (26 and 27), known to us from early photographs or other records, was preserved with equal intensity in the dried state (28). The special facial qualities of the Maori chief were carried to wood sculpture. The relationship of dried heads to some wooden masks is clearly evident when we compare them, e.g. the dried head (28) with the mask (29).

26 ◁
A portrait plaster of the face of the Ngati Whakatane-Te Arawa chief Taupua te Whanoa. This cast in the collections of the Dominion Museum, Wellington, is a copy of the original which was "taken from the living face" of Taupua-te-Whanoa in 1853 by the Rev Mr Fletcher, private secretary to Governor Grey. Sir George Grey presented the original cast to the British Museum and later General Gordon Robley, an enthusiastic student of tattoo (*moko*) and collector of dried heads, obtained this copy for his friend Gilbert Mair who in turn sent it to Elsdon Best for the Dominion Museum. Gilbert Mair described the chief in a letter to Elsdon Best as "a man of rank, a seer, and the designer and principal carver of the famous old house here" (Ohinemutu). The face illustrates the close relationship between actual faces and certain carved faces (compare 31). The dignity and power of expression and the deeply engraved and rhythmical tattoo of the living face and of the dried head were impressed on carved portrait heads.

27 ⇩

Polynesian facial features, characteristic expression, and the moulding effect of grooved tattoo, created in the old-time Maori a type that is unique to New Zealand. This 19th century photograph of the head of Tomaki-te-Mutu of Coromandel shows the usual combination of determination, ferocity and dignity seen in many portraits of Maori chiefs. The mummified head (28) preserves in death these qualities of the living face.

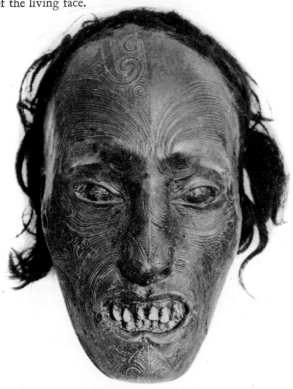

28 ⇧

Preserved head (*pakipaki*) of a long-dead chief which is now in the Saffron Walden Museum, Essex, England. This head, skilfully mummified by steaming, smoking and oiling processes, is life-size because the skull was left in it (for some reason the modern New Zealander insists on referring to such heads as "shrunken heads", which they are not). Dried heads were kept in villages and were seen often by carvers, who were naturally impressed by them. Their association with ancestral spirits and their relationship to the carved mask may be seen in (29) and in the many illustrations of portrait heads (e.g. 31, 102).

29 ⇩

Gable mask (*koruru*) with inlaid shell eyes. *Height:* 10½" (26.6cm). *Collection:* Municipal Museum of Ethnology, Cologne, West Germany.

This mask is placed below the photograph of the 19th century chief (27) and the mummified head (28), to allow direct visual comparison. This illustration, which could be supplemented by many more, sufficiently demonstrates the realistic relationship between the face of the old-time Maori chief and the portraits of wood sculpture.

35

◁ **30–31** (head detail) ⇧

An ancestral post image (*pou-tokomanawa*) made at Manutuke about 1860 by a carver named Timote Tohi (or Tuhi), originally for a house of Te Hauke, Hawke's Bay, and the well-known chief Te Haupuka, but retained by one Pitau. *Height:* 42″ (107cm). *Collection:* Hawke's Bay Museum, Napier.

The image is identified by an old script label on the back which reads: "Te Waaka Perohuka—a famous ancestor of the Rongowhakaata or Ngati Whaukauoue tribe—was a great fighting chief and went down to Wairoa and carried everything before him. This was carved by Timote Tohe at Manutuke about 1860 and was for a carved house that was being erected for Te Hapuka of Hawke's Bay—but was kept back by Pitau on account of it being his ancestor." An added note reads: "Got from Pitau November 1912 by G. J. Black."

The determination and forceful expression of the face (31) gives credence to the fighting skill of Te Waaka Perohuka as described in the words of the old label, but the author has not yet been able to link a chief by this name to any particular sequence of historical events. The strong character of the face is due as much to tattoo pattern as to form. Details of note are the hair which is tied as a topknot (*tikitiki*); and holes are drilled through the ear lobes to receive the ties of ornamental feather bundles or other ornaments.

Head with inset shell eyes, fringing hair eyelashes, and inlaid human incisor teeth, the lower three of which are missing. *Height:* 11⅝″ (29.5cm). *Collection:* British Museum, London.

This unusual and old head was presented to the British Museum by Sir George Grey. A manaia head, not visible from the frontal view illustrated, is set behind the crown. A hole cut in the base of the head measures about 4″ (10cm) deep by 2⅜″ (6cm) round and appears to have been used to receive a supporting peg. As dried heads were often displayed on a stake, and as there are records of the substitution of wooden versions of dried heads for lost or destroyed originals, it is probable that this head is a wooden substitute for a dried head. The style of portraiture and the use of human teeth in the mouth and the hair eyelashes support this tentative identification.

⇩ **32**

37

33 ⇧
Mask from Okarea pa, Whirinaki River, above Te Waiti.
Height: 25″ (64cm). *Collection:* Otago Museum, Dunedin.

The mask was found in pieces near the main entrance of
Okarea pa and was probably part of a gateway. It has a
rather sinister and threatening expression which is augmented
by the pierced eyes and mouth which provide a dramatic
effect, especially when such a head is viewed against a bright
night sky or under certain daylight conditions. The face is
flattened and squared to fit into the architectural arrangement
for which it was designed.

⇩ **34**
Slab with two chiefly male heads and a noble female head set
with attendant manaia. *Dimensions:* 1′10″ × 2′5¾″ (56cm ×
76cm). *Collection:* Dominion Museum, Wellington.

This carving was well documented by Augustus Hamilton
in his *Maori Art*, Wellington, 1896, who stated its origin
simply: "This fine slab was carved, for the purpose of
illustrating this work [*Maori Art*] by Tene, of Rotoehu, at
Rotorua, and shows the details of designs better than on a
dried head."

Pou-tokomanawa are supporting the middle portion of a house ridge-beam. The term is also used for façade ridge support posts when they are present, as in (35). Images are usually incorporated in these posts and there is a tradition that these figures represent primal canoe ancestors who stand to greet all who enter a house. Structurally the *pou-tokomanawa* is designed to take the downward thrust of the ridge-beam, which may weigh many tons in the largest 19th century houses. This function explains in part their squat stance and massive modelling. *Pou-tokomanawa* are generally of the "naturalistic" or "portrait" type (for example 30, 37). The size of the figure is a fair indication of the size of the house it came from. As a general rule images grow taller and heavier as the 19th century progresses (e.g. from figures of 3' (37) to figures of about 6' (38)). Almost all ancestral images removed from houses have had the upper post and lower earth footing cut off.

35 ◁

A meeting-house at Puatia which was built, according to the artist George French Angas, by a chief of Otawhao to commemorate the conquest of Maketu, Bay of Plenty. The façade of this house is typical of conventional Classic houses although the carvings set in the earth along the exterior wall are of extraordinary form. The forward support post is of the *pou-tokomanawa* type. From a lithograph in *The New Zealanders Illustrated*, London, 1846.

36 ◁

Interior of a meeting-house, East Coast district, showing support images in a house of modern origin. As houses grew in size *pou-tokomanawa* increased not only in height but also in number. The clothing of post images with cloaks is often seen in houses today, yet there is no evidence to indicate that this dressing is an old custom.

▷ **37**

A small ridge-support image (*pou-tokomanawa*). *Height:* 36" (91cm). *Collection:* Hawke's Bay Museum, Napier.

   This image, of small size and obvious age, has escaped the fate of being painted red. The original colour of wood richly patinated by time and handling enhances its impressive sculptural quality. Spirals mark the knees, and tattoo (*moko*) ornaments the face and buttocks. All surface decoration is applied with great delicacy. The hands possess four fingers and a thumb. This image compares in form closely with the free-standing figures (42–43, 44).

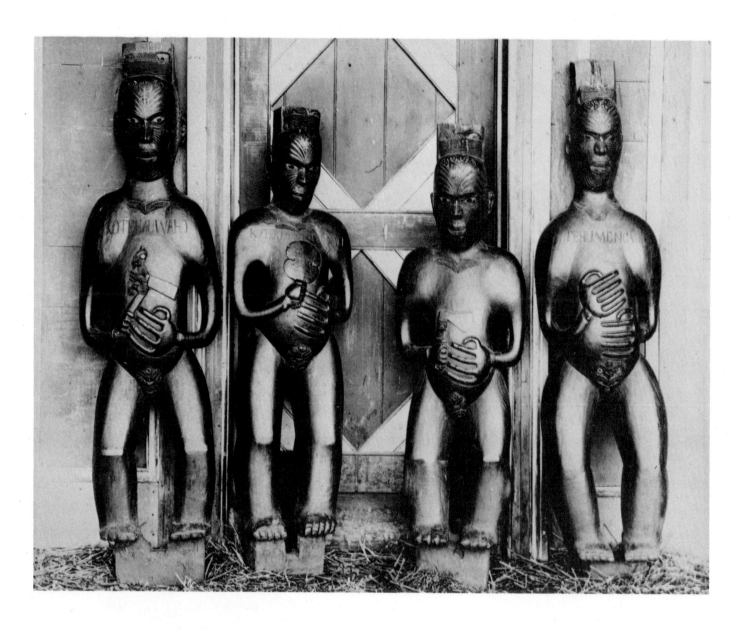

38 ⇧

Four of a group of ancestral ridge-support images (*pou-tokomanawa*) from a house which formerly stood at Redcliffs near Taradale, Hawke's Bay. *Collection:* Hawke's Bay Museum, Napier.

This old photograph is dated 1889. Some of these figures originally stood in line supporting the single main ridge within the Redcliffs meeting-house but were removed before this house was destroyed by fire. However there is no evidence that all four figures came from this one house. Large five-finger hands, the presence of carved tomahawk, names cut in Roman letters on breasts, and the large size, classify this group within the period of Modern *pou-tokomanawa*.

FREE-STANDING TIKI

⇩ **39–40–41**

Three views of a free-standing image. *Height:* 17¾″ (45cm). W. O. Oldman *Collection,* Dominion Museum.

This male image, of vigorous form, formerly had hair tied to the head in the manner of 42–43, 44, the evidence being the hair attachment holes on crown and back of head. A post-European date of manufacture is ascribable on the basis of the style, as the eye slits are designed to hold sealing-wax, which remains intact. The deep channel at back and the holes on shoulder and stomach are old tunnels left by the lavae of the *huhu* beetle (*Prinophis reticularus*). Old and naturally seasoned woods were often used by the carver, who disregarded minor imperfections if the material was otherwise suitable for a particular job. The head, which is very large in relation to the body, is delicately incised with facial tattoo (*moko*) while the buttocks are decorated with spiral patterns.

Images of a unique type are here described as free-standing because they are three-dimensional, they are not designed for house attachment, and they are proportioned and balanced to stand freely on the floor. Adzed cuts are found on the soles of their feet and indicate they were not sawn from a post or house as in the case with some *tekoteko* and post images (e.g. 151–152). In the mid-1950s, when the author was studying in England, he traced a series of images of a distinctive free-standing type which share common characteristics such as size, three-dimensional form, and human hair attached to the head (or, when the hair is missing, attachment points for hair may be observed). This unusual type which had disappeared from New Zealand until the return of a specimen in the W. O. Oldman Collection in 1948, is represented here by three specimens: 39–41, 42–43, and 44.

The type was first defined in the literature of Maori carving in a volume honouring Dr H. D. Skinner entitled *Anthropology in the South Seas* (see Bibliography, Barrow, 1959). Five were presented in this paper as a new type, and the suggestion made that they were god images similar to the small portable gods found widely in Polynesia, especially in Tahiti. Dr Skinner, in a letter to the author after the publication of the book, made the suggestion that these small tiki were not god images but house-post images of an early contact period when houses were small and before the time of incorporation of images into *pou-tokomanawa*. This latter interpretation seems valid. Even in some modern houses the ancestral image is placed loosely in front of the ridge support post and not carved in the post. The task of carving a large figure as part of a slender post requires great labour and large wastage of timber.

42–43 ⇦
Two views of a free-standing image. *Height:* 17¾″ (45cm).
Collection: Glasgow Art Gallery and Museum, Kelvingrove,
Glasgow, Scotland.

This example of the small free-standing image compares in
type with (39–40–41 and 44). It embodies all the characteristic
features of this series which had disappeared from New
Zealand collections, but had been retained in early English
collections. According to a family tradition this image was
collected and brought to England by a Royal Navy mid-
shipman named Samuel Folker. Thereafter the family tradition is in error, possibly through confusion with another
item collected by Folker for it claims ". . . the idol was stolen
from the Windward Island, West Indies", and "the middies
were followed by natives who shot poisoned arrows at them".
A striking feature of this figure is the skill of surface adze-
work which, significantly, continues on the underside of the
feet. The form relates in general proportions to the massive
East Coast stockade figure (147–148).

⇨ **44**
Free-standing image. *Height:* 15¾″ (40cm). *Collection:* Hun-
terian Museum of the University of Glasgow, Glasgow,
Scotland.

No history of this outstanding carving is recorded other
than in its museum accession data, which were entered before
1900. Large circlets of serrated *paua* (*Haliotis iris*) are inset as
eyes. Surface decoration is limited to a few lines to represent
facial tattoo (*moko*), while some anatomical features such as
kneecaps, umbilicus and breastbone are carved in low relief.
The ear plugs, one of which has been mended with a bent
piece of split supplejack vine, appear designed to take
ornamental feather bundles. The human hair tied to the head
is abundant and well preserved.

This particular image of the free-standing type can be
closely compared with certain Hawaiian images which have
hair attached to their heads. The Hawaiian images of similar
type seem related to the New Zealand images, so it is not
unreasonable to postulate a common ancestor in the period
before the forebears of the Maori and of the Hawaiians parted
in search of new islands.

THE LIZARD MOTIF

THE LIZARD MOTIF is generally rare in Maori carving art yet it is relatively common in Bay of Plenty carving. Maori religious ideas relating to the lizard are ancient and complex, not adequately recorded, and elusive to modern enquiry. Dr H. D. Skinner in his paper *Crocodile and Lizard in New Zealand Myth and Material Culture* (1964) presents a convincing case relating folk memories of crocodiles of South-East Asian homelands, with the fear of lizards in New Zealand, and folk beliefs concerning the saurian *taniwha* or water-monster which lurked in deep river pools and on certain parts of the sea coast. Generally lizards were regarded as emissaries of Whiro, who personified death and disease. It was held that the gods sometimes used a lizard to destroy a man by having it enter his body to eat away his vital organs. In carving art, lizards served mainly as tapu marks (for example, on the sacred thwart of a canoe), and thus they served as guardians to good, as well as evil forces. The paper by Elsdon Best entitled *Notes on the Occurrence of the Lizard in Maori Carvings, and various Myths and Superstitions connected with Lizards,* 1923, (see Bibliography) provides detailed material on this subject.

45 ◁

A pair of downward-facing lizards are conspicuous on the frontal ridge-support post of the house Nuku-te-Apiapi which formerly stood at Whakarewarewa, Rotorua. This house, which was carved in the late 1800s at Matata in the Bay of Plenty, was not erected until about 1900 because of a series of misfortunes relating to it. As a result of these ominous events it stood for many years neglected and gradually falling into a dilapidated condition. After World War II it was purchased by the Internal Affairs Department and was later transferred, its panels finding their way to the board room of the Arawa Trust Office, Rotorua. Their refurbishment there with modern red paint made them look cleaner, but has detracted from their general appearance as works of Maori art.

46 ↻

A pair of lizards from the sliding door panel of the Bay of Plenty house named Nuku-te-Apiapi (45). The entire front panel of the door from which this detail was taken is illustrated, the lizards detailed here being a small area between the legs of the central mythological figure (49). Recognisable renderings of the lizard are found in both early and late period sculpture although they seem to have increased in frequency during the latter half of the 19th century. The form of the lizard is usually adapted to the space available on post, panel, or box (compare 47–48).

47–48 ⬎
Front and side views of a bone-chest (*waka-tupapaku*) with manaia-headed lizard forming the basic design. *Height:* 48″ (122cm). *Collection:* Auckland Institute and Museum, Auckland.

This box, which came from a cave at Waimamaku, Northland, served as a receptacle for the bones of a person of rank. The lizard here appears as a protective guardian.

Door panel from the Bay of Plenty house Nuku-te-Apiapi (45) with design composed of central fabulous figure which combines physical elements of bird, man, and reptile. The lizards set between the legs are elsewhere enlarged in detail (46). The head of the central figure is that of a conventional manaia of Arawa style, as are the several supplementary manaia. Secondary manaia and interlocking spirals fill in the areas not occupied by the central image, in the usual manner of Bay of Plenty-East Coast styles.

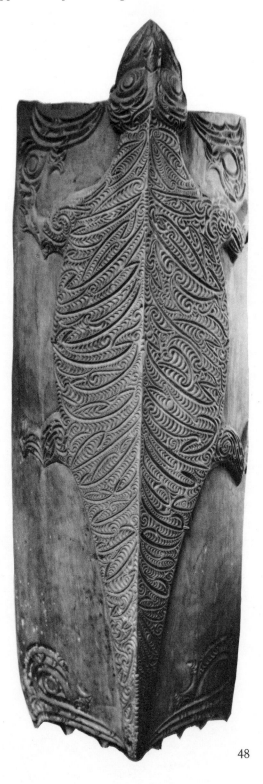

THE *Marakihau*

The *marakihau* is defined in Williams's *A Dictionary of the Maori Language* as "a fabulous sea monster", thus it is a kind of *taniwha*, which is in turn described by Williams as "a fabulous monster supposed to reside in deep water". In physical form the *marakihau* combines the features of both man and fish and is thus a kind of merman or mermaid. According to legend *marakihau* had a tubelike tongue (*ngongo*) through which they could suck fish or a whole canoe with men and cargo. The appearance of *marakihau* as ancestral panels stems from the belief that some men were transformed to *taniwha* at death.

50 ⬁

A *marakihau* panel from a meeting-house of Maketu built in the 19th century. *Dimensions:* 93″ (236cm) × 24″ (61cm). *Collection:* Bernice P. Bishop Museum, Honolulu.

The tube tongue (*ngongo*) of the *marakihau*, which is conventionally depicted in the act of sucking a fish, is missing from this carving. Spinal triangles found on *marakihau* of the 19th century represent the dorsal fins of fish, while late decadent and folksy versions quite delightfully represent western mermaids (118). Creatures that may be identified as *marakihau* in Classic carving are few in number and mainly found in Classic North Auckland carving of the Contact period. The North Auckland treasure-box (221) presents a good example of pre-Contact *marakihau*. Sinuous bodies and webbed feet are their most significant characteristics.

THE *Marakihau*

51 ⇧
The house Te Tokanganui-a-Noho as photographed by Muir and Moodie of Dunedin about the turn of the century. It stands to this day at the town of Te Kuiti. Originally it was built by the followers of Te Kooti Rirangi then presented to the Ngati-Maniapoto in appreciation of hospitality given to Te Kooti during the years of his harassment by pursuing Government forces between 1872 and 1883. Te Tokanganui-a-Noho has in its porch some of the finest extant 19th century *marakihau* panels (52, 53).

THE *Marakihau*

⇗ 53

The same *marakihau* panels as illustrated in (52) are here shown in the 20th century picture with a late paint cover, a change which has much detracted from the charm of the early paintwork seen in the early photograph. Restoration and "improvement" of Maori houses often spoils the effectiveness of the carvings as is clearly seen when we compare the change in appearance of dignified old carvings that have been given a kind of misguided facelift. This is not only a Maori failing. It has happened to certain museum specimens under the control of men who should give guidance rather than set a bad example. Conservation means preservation, strengthening and cleaning, but without substantially changing appearance or hiding the dignity of age and beauty of patina.

52 ⇗

A 19th century photograph showing the two *marakihau* panels in the porch of Te-Tokanganui-a-Noho (51) at a time when they were still embedded in earth. The old red, black, and white paintwork, presumably the original coat, has been painted over on one or two occasions.

54 ⇧

A water-colour by Augustus Earle of a storehouse at Kororareka (Russell), Bay of Islands. *Collection:* Rex K. de Nan Kivell.

Augustus Earle, who was born in England in 1798, arrived in New Zealand in 1827. His drawings are among the best and the earliest of graphic records of Maori life. A second foodstore (*pataka*) drawn by Earle appears at (153).

THE *Pakake* MOTIF

A common bargeboard motif found on North Island storehouses is that commonly called a whale (*pakake*) although Pine Taiapa (80) believes it is a kind of sea monster (*taniwha*). The symbolical meaning of this creature has been forgotten. It may well be a *taniwha*, but the physical form of the creature is obviously based on what a whale (56), with fluke traditionally set to apex of the bargeboard (*maihi*) and head to the lower end (54). In the oldest carvings with this motif, figures are sometimes depicted hauling this *pakake* (55). The head and jaws are commonly rendered in sweeping spiral forms such as on the Te Kaha foodstore board (55) which is illustrated in enlarged detail (57). There is no evidence that the Maori could catch whales. In pre-Contact times, before whaler days, a whale cast ashore was regarded as a piece of good luck as it provided abundance of flesh and bone. Tribal arguments have arisen over the right to possess the carcass of a stranded whale. The appearance of the *pakake* motif on storehouses suggests they were regarded as symbols of abundance and prosperity.

55–56 ⇨

A foodstore board with whale (*pakake*) design from a large storehouse (*pataka*) which is believed to have stood at Te Kaha near East Cape about 1780. *Length:* 12' (366cm). *Collection:* Auckland Museum.

According to the *Annual Report of the Auckland Museum*, 1911–12, the set of *pataka* carving of which this board is a part was, in the year 1814, "secreted in a cave in order to save them from a raid of the Ngapuhi Maoris led by the well-known chief, Morenga. There they remained until 1900, when they were purchased from the Maoris by Mr Spencer, of Auckland, from whom the Museum has now acquired them." The flowing rhythmical movement of the images is as fine as may be found in any Maori wood sculpture. The *pakake* is obscured by overlaid figures, both manaia and tiki, which haul it by a "rope" of small figures joined by sexual copulation. The line drawing (56) will aid the eye in following the outline of the whale form on the *maihi* (55).

(detail of design) **57** ⇨

Detail of (55) showing the head of the whale (*pakake*) rendered with large eye and massive curvilinear style tongue and jaws. A large outward-turned manaia terminates the lower, while numerous supplementary figures are worked into a tracery as background pattern. This detail study also reveals the masterly surface decoration which is basically the zigzag or water motif termed *tara-tara-a-kai*. This surface is also found in certain canoe parts and some stockade posts.

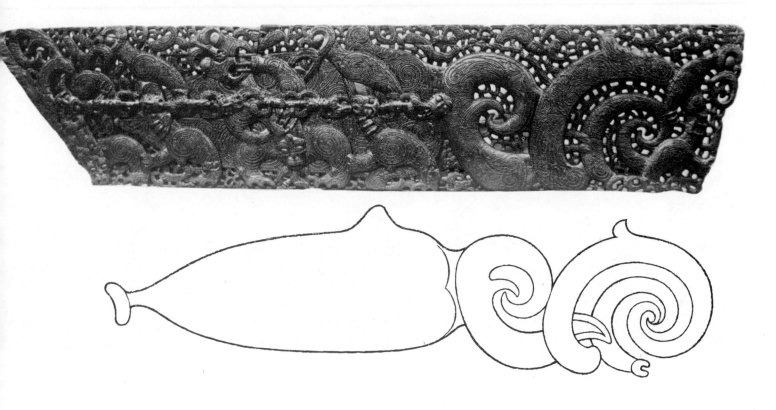

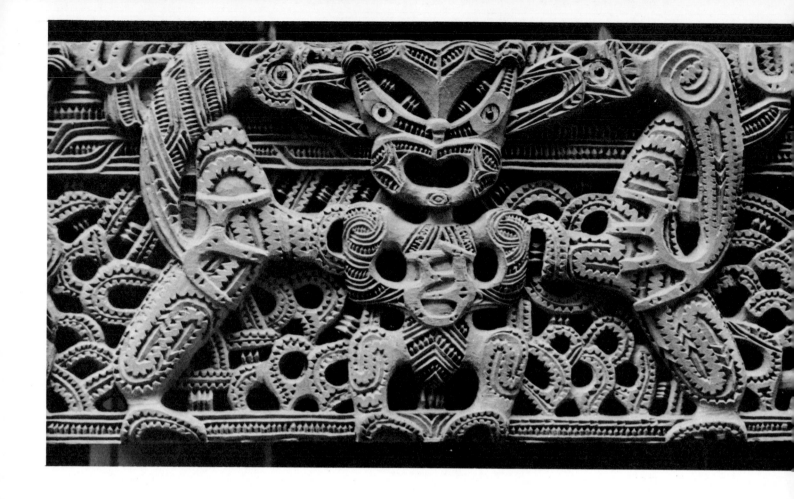

FOLLOWING THE HUMAN IMAGE (tiki) the manaia is the motif of subsequent importance in wood sculpture. What manaia is, nobody knows for certain. Some experts claim to know but base their confidence merely on the theory that the manaia is a human form viewed in profile.

The author's interpretation here stated is tentative but it emerges from a search for comparative material from other parts of the Pacific, the actual study of the physical form of manaia, and relevant Maori religious and social ideas. A statement of the position of this book in interpreting manaia is given in the Introduction, page 20.

Most manaia have characteristics that suggest bird inspiration while in some of its forms it is a true bird-man (68, 69). Reptilian elements also occur in relation to it (49). Generally birds and reptiles are closely associated in primitive reasoning, and in fact by zoologists. Some Maori descriptions of fabulous monsters (taniwha) reinforces reptilian association. Positive evidence of bird-man forms in Polynesia (including New Zealand) was published in a paper entitled *Material Evidence of the Bird-man Concept in Polynesia* (see Bibliography, Barrow, 1967). The author there postulates that manaia in many of its forms is a bird-man, and that most New Zealand human images (tiki) have superimposed avian features, of varying degrees. This idea does not confuse the clear difference between manaia and tiki, but it does suggest the hybridisation of forms. This interpretation is used in various captions and is clearly acknowledged in the Introduction.

⇧ 58

Detail of the manaia-tiki combination on the baseboard (*paepae*) of the Te Oha storehouse (*pataka*) which is in the Maori Hall of the Auckland Institute and Museum.

It illustrates the basic manaia-tiki relationship both of classic form and "behaviour". The pattern is based on the theme of central ancestral image with manaia "bird-men" reaching to a central figure. This arrangement is sometimes assymetrical, with a single manaia approaching the human figure (64, 65, 66), but the manaia-tiki relationship is basic. This Te Oha storehouse detail showing tiki and paired manaia has been widely used as a theme motif for the decoration on several publications, including several *Dominion Museum Monographs* by Elsdon Best, Augustus Hamilton's *Maori Art,* and the author's *Decorative Arts of the New Zealand Maori* (see Bibliography).

59 ⇨
Image on a ridge-beam. *Height:* lower figure, 3′5½″ (105cm); the other, 3′4½″ (102.9cm). *Collection:* Dominion Museum, Wellington.

The bird association of this type of figure is confined by traditional Maori explanation of their avian inspiration and the evidence of our own eyes. The Koururu and *ruru* motif, of which this carving is a good representative example, is evidently related in facial form to the owl (*ruru*) which was an important omen bird and carrier of spirits (the *ruru* motif is similar to Koururu but the latter has two points as the crown representing feather tufts). Elsdon Best in his classic two-volume work entitled *The Maori* records a Maori legend in which Rongo, who acquired the art of carving by supernatural means, used Koururu (the personified form of owl) as a sacred offering and buried his body under the rear wall of the house. (The story is told in the Introduction, page 21.) For this reason, the Maori tells us, many carvings have the burning staring eyes of Koururu. In this symbol both human and bird elements are fused to form a kind of bird-man.

60 ⇦
Detail from the upper end of the handle of a ceremonial adze (*toki-pu-tangata*). K. A. Webster *Collection.* See page 142, and the specimen 196, for information of this type of adze. The head detailed here is unmistakably birdlike and is related to the form of Koururu (59). The mouth in this head strongly resembles the beak of a seabird, though the general character of the face is owlish. This is a good three-dimensional example of human and bird elements combined to compose a fabulous bird-man creature. Although it is not specifically a *manaia* in physical form it is a close relation and in metaphysical meaning it was probably also related.

61 ⇧

Gable mask of distinctive East Coast style (compare the head of the Manutuke panel, 110). *Height:* 15¼″ (38.8cm). *Collection:* National Museum, Dublin.

This mask, which is of excellent quality, is believed to have been collected during Cook's voyages. The face is basically human, yet the eyes are glaring and birdlike as the Maori tradition of Koururu explains (see Introduction page 21, and caption to 59). The surface spiral treatment is flowing, with extremely sensitive chisel work. Ear plugs are as yet unrecorded from Classic culture, yet they are represented on carving and especially on carvings from the East Coast (for example. see panel 106). The ear plug may have been used in old New Zealand but its appearance in carving is traditional, vestigial, and possibly a relic of the pre-New Zealand Maori. Cook and other early observers noted many objects thrust through holes in the ears of Maoris, but none recorded ear plugs.

⇩ **62–63**

A small bone-chest (*waka-tupapaku*). *Height:* 18″ (45.7cm). *Collection:* Dominion Museum, Wellington.

This box has a shallow cavity in the back, measuring 6″ × 3⅜″ and ¾″ deep, which was intended to accommodate relics such as small bones, hair, or teeth. The hollow part was formerly closed over by a rebated lid which has been lost. The lower part of the end is decayed but comparative evidence suggests the lost part was in the form of a solid peg by which the box could be stood upright on the floor of a cave (compare 13). Strong traces of red ochre (*kokowai*) coating remain on the head and body.

The special value of the box from the point of view of interpretation of wood sculpture form is the undoubted avaian features superimposed on a basically human form. The mouth and eyes are decidedly bird-inspired, but even more so are the upper and lower parts of the arms and the claw-like hands, which resemble in form the lower limbs of a ground bird. Each of the three figures on each hand is a talon and not a human finger, which elsewhere in Maori wood sculpture is clearly rendered.

64 ⇦
Unfinished side panel (*pakitara*), from a small storehouse (*pataka*), at the "blocked-out" stage of carving (see page 72). *Dimensions:* 35″ (89cm) × 16″ (40.7cm). W. O. Oldman *Collection*, Dominion Museum, Wellington.

Carried to England with (65), this slab probably belongs to the same storehouse as the slab (64). The manaia and tiki movement is to the right in (64) and to the left in (65) which supports the proposition that they were originally intended to form complimentary sides of the same storehouse.

65 ⇦
Finished side panel (*pakitara*) from a small storehouse (*pataka*). *Dimensions:* 51″ (130cm) × 15″ (38cm). W. O. Oldman *Collection:* Dominion Museum, Wellington.

This fine small side panel was carried to England by Admiral Sir Michael Seymour of Cardlington with the related side panel (64), at some time before the death of the Admiral in 1850. Both carry the alternate manaia-tiki design also found on storehouse frontal baseboards (*paepae*) (66), and on the side walls of late period *pataka* (160). The pair of boards (64–65), which appear to have been collected in a manufacturing phase, serve as valuable illustrative material on carving technique (see pages 71–73). As art they present an unrivalled beauty as found in a low-relief wood sculpture.

66 ⇨
Details of the manaia and tiki of a baseboard (*paepae*) from a Bay of Plenty storehouse named Te Takinga, which is now in the Dominion Museum, Wellington.

The central figure in this detail is flanked by two large manaia which both face to the right and each toward the tiki they relate to. A secondary manaia of small size and of fragmented type is set below the beak of the left manaia and it "bites" at the upraised hand of the centre image. The Te Takinga storehouse, which has had a very varied career, was exhibited in England and latterly stood for many years at the edge of Lake Papaitonga on the property of Sir Walter Buller, KCMG. Sir Walter was its last owner before it entered the collection of the Dominion Museum. There is a tradition that Te Takinga was made from the hull of one of the war canoes drawn thirty miles overland from Maketu by the Nga Puhi warrior Hongi Hika for his attack on Mokoia Island, Lake Rotorua, in 1822.

67

Manaia-ornamented comb, with broken teeth, excavated from a swamp site at Kauri Point at the western end of the Bay of Plenty. *Height:* 3" (7.6cm). *Collection:* Department of Anthropology, Auckland University.

About three hundred combs or comb fragments were found in this site. One of the finest recoveries was the comb illustrated at (20). The excavation of decorated wooden objects under conditions of archaeological control, the relation of them to layers (strata), and subjection of samples to Carbon 14 analysis, provides reliable dating of comb types and thus to the sequence of Prehistoric carving style in that region. Specifically these combs give firm evidence of the development of Classic type manaia by mid-16th century. Mr Wilfred Shawcross of Auckland University directed the Kauri Point excavation as described in the *Journal of the Polynesian Society* (see Bibliography). Careful analysis of this material in relation to stratigraphic data and the Carbon 14 tests indicated that combs early in time tended to have rectangular outlines (67) while the upper levels produced combs of rounded and more elaborate shape (for example (20) is classified as the late developed type). Delicate manaia decorations confirm the early existence of manaia that serve as precursors of the manaia heads found on the side of combs collected in the Historic period by Cook and other visitors of the late 18th century (see 200).

68 ⇧
Manaia are best seen when isolated from the general design of a carving. This photographic cut-out is of a manaia on an East Coast panel (*poupou*). The entire carving may be seen in the illustration of a wall to Te Mana-o-Turanga (109) where the manaia is standing on a knee of the ancestral figure, in the left panel. The manaia is one of bird-man type, complete with horned beak and claw hand, with a manaia head overlaying the centre of the torso. The strange horn on the beak is a convention of bird renderings in several Oceanic and South-East Asian areas and has appeared on New Zealand manaia since at least the mid-16th century (67).

69 ⇦
Cut-out detail of a manaia, from the hull of a ceremonial canoe which was formerly in the possession of K. A. Webster and is now in the P. Ludwig *Collection,* Cologne Municipal Museum of Ethnology, Cologne, West Germany.

The distinctive features of full manaia are well represented by this example of manaia, which compares well with (68) and (70) as a typical bird-man type. The head is round and small with large round eye (in this example the eye is inlaid with a circlet of shell), the mouth is a beak with a horn or spur surmounting it (a feature sometimes excluded in drawings made by scientists), it has a V-tongue, a three-fingered hand, and a body with both upper and lower limbs. It is highly improbable that such manaia are merely side renderings of the human figure, regardless of the general acceptance of this idea. Manaia must not be studied from the preconceived European rule that two manaia heads make a full-face human mask. This device is used by Maori craftsmen but in such instances the work seems derived from two manaia rather than the manaia derived from the central division of a mask, as so postulated.

63

70 ⇧
Isolated manaia detail from a door lintel (*pare*) in the British
Museum which was collected in 1869 by Capt. J. P. Luce, RN,
when he was in command of HMS *Esk*.

This detail shows one of a pair of major manaia which are
both placed facing a central tiki in characteristic relationship.
The small head and horned and toothed beak compare well
with manaia (69), although in this manaia the V tongue is
absent but a "tooth" is present. Manaia is one of the most
diverse of sculpture symbols and one of the most ingeniously
adapted to various arrangements. Its appearance as whole
bird-men or as the head on a snakelike or fish body or as part
of the hand of an ancestral image make any single identification with one creature quite impossible. Manaia is elusive and
mysterious and probably served as a symbol of supernatural
force, especially mana, which the name manaia suggests.

72 ⇨
Detail from the underside of the treasure-box (*wakahuia*).
Collection: British Museum, London.

This fine box reached England on one of the ships of Capt.
James Cook. The abundant manaia are of unusual form. They
surround four ancestral figures which are arranged on the
base alternately top and bottom as seen in a view of the whole
underside of this box (219). Basically each manaia is merely a
head, which resembles that of a gull and is formed by a kind
of figure-of-eight design, open on the beak side with a shell
eye-circlet inlaid in some heads but not in all.

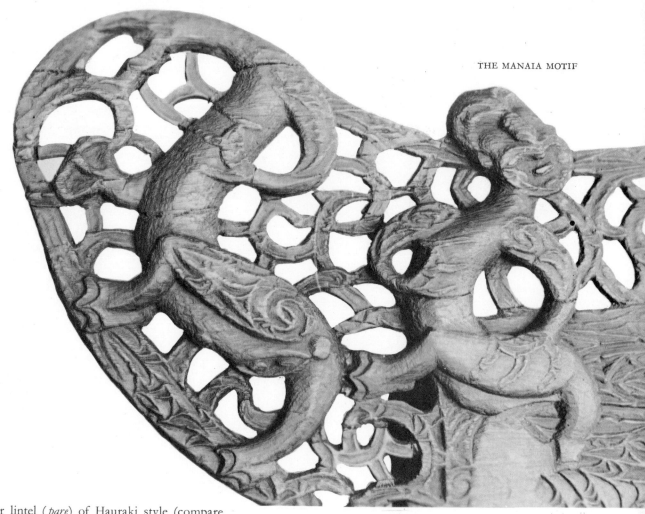

71 ⇨

Left side of a door lintel (*pare*) of Hauraki style (compare *pare* 123). *Collection:* Alexander Museum, Wanganui.

The large out-turned manaia grasps and holds in its mouth or bites the tail of a manaia-headed creature of legless body and snakelike appearance. Sexual organs are rarely found on manaia, and very rarely female sexual organs such as seen on this manaia.

73-74 ⇧ ⇨
Canoe bailer (*tata*) collected on one of Cook's voyages.
Length: 20″ (51cm). *Collection:* British Museum, London.

This bailer offers further evidence of the probable association of manaia and birds. Seen as a whole this bailer looks
like a floating seabird of graceful neck. The detail of the
handle (74) reinforces the impression that the form is inspired
by a bird and not, as many experts would insist, merely a
human head in profile. The presence of a mound or notch
on the beak, which is often rendered as a horn or spur as
in (68, 69), is an old feature of manaia as noted in relation to
the manaia head on the Kauri Point comb (67).

75 ⇨
Manaia head at the upper end of a canoe paddle. *Collection:*
British Museum, London.

The manaia was a favourite handle termination and is
found, for example, on paddles, as pommels on short weapons
(185–188), and at the end of bailer handles (see 73–74).

76 ⟲

Canoe prow (*tau-ihu*) from Mokau, North Taranaki. *Collection:* Taranaki Museum, New Plymouth.

This prow, a rare specimen of Taranaki craftsmanship, conforms in image and spiral arrangement to the standard canoe prow composition of Classic times, in having namely, forward-facing and aft-facing figures with an intermediate central figure balanced on either side by interlocking spirals. This unusual Taranaki prow appears to predate Classic, of which (178) serves as a good Taranaki example. The line analysis (77) reveals distinctive manaia type images (excluding the stern-facing tiki) with bodies that link tails to form simple interlocking spirals. A comparison of photograph and line drawing shows graphically that strengthening joiners or chocks are not intrinsically part of the basic design but are a technical device used by carvers to secure strength over fretted areas. The presence of these "connectors" confuses the untrained eye and hides the design from most people who are unfamiliar with Maori carving.

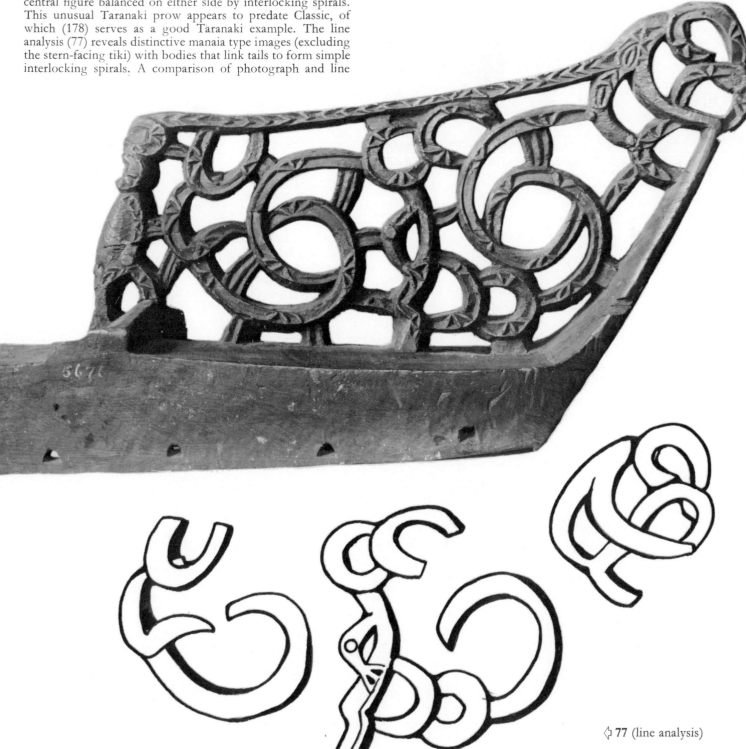

⟲ **77** (line analysis)

Anaha te Rahui, one of the last of the great master wood-carvers (*tohunga-whakairo-rakau*), who died in 1913 at about the age of eighty. A carver of Arawa tradition and lore, Anaha claimed descent from Ngatoroirangi the high priest of the Arawa canoe, and he included in his aristocratic genealogy many master carvers. Two nephews, Neke Kapua and Tene Waitere, were among his male relatives who carried the family chisel (*whao*) into modern times. The Dominion Museum has in its collection a set of fifteen small panels carved by Anaha at the request of Augustus Hamilton in 1905. These panels were published by W. J. Phillipps in 1941 (see Bibliography) and they form a good basic pattern-range of 19th century Arawa carving tradition.

◁ 79

Te Whitireia house, one of the finest of 20th century carved houses (*whare whakairo*), was completed in 1939 at Whangara, on the East Coast. An ancestral panel (*poupou*) from the front porch is illustrated (81). This house was carved by Pine Taiapa (80) and assisting carvers of the Rotorua School of Maori Arts and Crafts which was established in the 1920s to aid the revival of carving art. Te Whitireia is modelled on Te Hau-ki-Turanga (101) of Manutuke which is now preserved in the Dominion Museum, Wellington. Pine Taiapa regards this house as the best of many houses he has designed and worked on, and it is also of great significance to him personally because of the symbolical importance of Whangara as a spiritual centre to the Ngati Porou, the tribe to which Pine Taiapa belongs.

CARVERS AND CARVING TECHNIQUE

Traditionally the sacred art of the Maori carver was maintained throughout the centuries by a succession of masters working within tribes, sub-tribes, and the individual families who specialised in carving art. These men respected many taboos, and lived up to a code of secrecy and professional exclusiveness. Today few esoteric rules remain: women, who were in former times rigidly excluded, are now permitted to watch carvers at work; many men will eat and smoke near uncompleted carvings; and some carvers will even blow shavings off unfinished work and dispose of shavings carelessly.

The Maori term for wood carving as a craft is simply *whakairo-rakau; whakairo* is a word for carved work in general whether in wood, bone, or stone, while *rakau* means wood, the material used. All high specialists were referred to as *tohunga*, so the master carver was called a *tohunga-whakairo-rakau*. As the important arts were followed by men of social rank who followed strict codes in relation to their arts, a religious association was natural and the highest craftsman were regarded as priests of a kind. Religion and life were one in old Polynesia and the practice of any art was controlled by tradition. Far from restricting craftsmen, the impersonal background to craft removed the need for eccentric individualism in work. Society was both critical and appreciative but any special achievement of the craftsman was said to come by the power of *mana* (spiritual power) rather than by personal effort.

◁ 80

The carving master (*tohunga-whakairo-rakau*) Pine Taiapa photographed at Tikitiki, 1965, when the author stayed as a guest in his house. Since Pine Taiapa left Te Aute college over half a century ago he has designed and worked on many carved houses with assisting teams working in the communal Maori way. Houses in the East Coast-Bay of Plenty region, and as far afield as Wellington and Taranaki, have been built or restored by the adze and chisel of Pine Taiapa and the men working under his supervision. At Waitangi he directed the building of the house erected to commemorate the signing of the Treaty of Waitangi. He always worked in close collaboration with Sir Apirana Ngata who, with other Maori leaders, inspired the vigorous revival of Maori arts from about the turn of the century. The central strengths of Pine Taiapa and of his younger brother Hone Taiapa OBE are insistence on good technique and dependence on traditional sources for inspiration.

CARVERS AND CARVING TECHNIQUE

⬐81
Steel-cut porch panel of the Whitireia house (79). Whitireia was modelled on Te Hau-ki-Turanga (101), and this panel may be compared closely to the Manatuke panels (e.g. 103, 104, 106) which are of the same inspiration. Te Hau-ki-Turanga, Te Mana-o-Turanga, and Whitireia are all products of the steel-tool era and of the Gisborne carving tradition; the first-named preceded the second by some thirty years, and Whitireia was carved some sixty years later than Te-Mana-o-Turanga.

82 ⬑
A fine old pinnacle figure (*tekoteko*). *Height:* 33½" (80.5cm) × 5" (12.7cm). W. O. Oldman *Collection*, Dominion Museum, Wellington.

Oldman's record of this *tekoteko* indicates it was taken to England in the South Sea London Missionary Society ship *Duff* by Capt. James Wilson (1798). The *Duff* did not call at New Zealand, but "curios" were often exchanged by sailors, and it is probable Captain Wilson or his men picked up this carving from another ship at some port of call. This superb carving is probably stone-cut or at least earliest iron-tool work. It has a soft plastic quality observed only in the best Maori wood sculpture.

83 ⬑
An adze complete with handle, lashing and nephrite blade. *Length:* 22⅝" (57.5cm). *Collection:* Museum fur Volkerkunde, Berlin, West Germany. Collected by the Forsters of the *Resolution* on Cook's second voyage.

The stone adze was the basic tool of the craftsman, but of the thousands which formerly existed this is possibly the only surviving complete specimen from the first Contact period. Late haftings of old blades, and those with metal plane blades are found in many museum collections, but this Berlin specimen is probably unique.

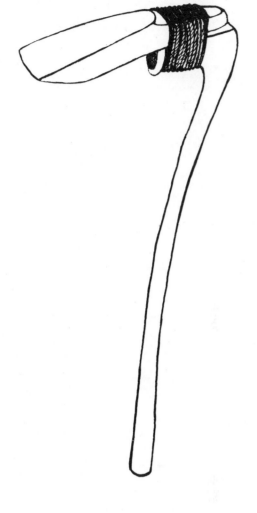

84 ⬑
A carver's mallet (*ta*). *Length:* 11" (28cm). *Collection:* Dominion Museum, Wellington.

Whalebone was the favourite mallet material of the wood-carver yet wooden mallets were also used and these were sometimes decorated. In this example the bruised surface area is where the mallet struck the chisel.

⬑85
A rare example of complete chisel (*whao*), complete with wooden handle, nephrite blade, and lashing, and recorded as having been collected by Captain Cook. *Overall length:* 8½" (21.5cm). *Collection:* British Museum, London.

Carving of the developed Classic kind went through stages as illustrated here by three manaia carvings prepared in 1949 by Mr I. C. Tuarau of the staff of the Dominion Museum, Wellington.

86

The craftsman grooved the intended design either wholly or in part as work progressed (see the early box illustrating this procedure 89–90). There is no reason to believe that old-time carvers drew their patterns before cutting. Some unfinished carvings show a few faint scratchlines or shallow grooves indicating the development of the surface decoration, but these apparently guided only the next immediate stage and outlined merely part of the whole design.

87 ⇦

The outlined design was then cut in low relief until the whole carving was "blocked-out" with the sculptural masses fully determined (see the storehouse boards 64, 65). The adze was the principal tool used at this stage of the work.

88 ⇦

Surface decoration was then added with small chisels and, where required, inlaid shell eyes were fitted by either pegging at the centre or fitting firmly over a central boss. Complete shells were occasionally inset as eyes, as in the Hauraki lintel (123), while the mask illustrated at (32) has hair, eyelashes and human teeth added to the face. Some finished carvings were painted with red ochre and shark-liver oil, but it is a mistake to imagine that all Maori carvings were red and a fallacy to believe that they all should be.

89 ⇧   90 ⇧   91 ⇧   92 ⇧

Carving procedures illustrated by four sides of an unfinished treasure-box (*wakahuia*). The views are unfinished side (89), unfinished top and rebated lid (90), finished underside (91), and finished side (92). *Length:* 15½″ (39cm). *Collection:* Hawke's Bay Museum, Napier.

The undersides of treasure-boxes were better carved than the other surfaces as in their stowage position the boxes were suspended from house rafters, and thus normally seen from below. For this reason carvers tended to finish the bottoms of boxes first, then work on the sides, then finally complete the top. There are always exceptions to general rules and some boxes are found decorated on the top and not on the bottom. As a large number of boxes were collected unfinished we must conjecture they were either released in trade or that the maker had died and no-one was prepared to continue another's labour for reasons of taboo.

73

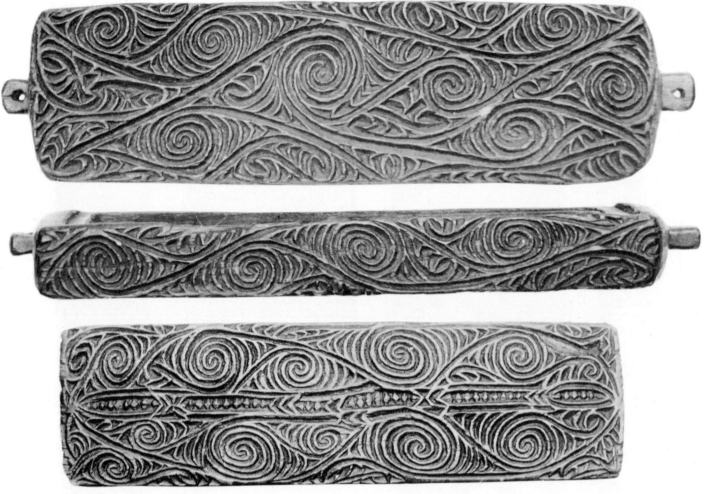

THE SPIRAL

93-94-95 ⇧
Three views of a completed feather-box (*wakahuia*). All the surfaces are covered by rich rhythmical spirals of a style which suggest a North Auckland provenience. The views are: base (93), side (94), and lid in isolation (95). *Length:* 15¾″ (40cm). *Collection:* Pitt Rivers Museum, Oxford, England. Museum records indicate that the box was taken to England early in the 19th century by a Captain Tupper of the Royal Navy.

96 ⇖
Details of a prow (*tau-ihu*) of the type associated with the war canoe (*waka-taua*). *Diameter of the spiral,* 15″ (38cm).

This massive interlocking spiral of pierced technique is cut with such sharp precision that it was probably carved with tempered steel tools. A highly stylised human image stands between this spiral and a second of equal size which is partly seen on left. The prow belonged to a canoe which helped convey the Atiawa people back to Taranaki from Waikanae in 1848.

97 ⇨
Side view of a feeding funnel (*koropata*). *Height:* 5⅛″ (13cm). *Diameter:* 8″ (20.3cm). *Collection:* London Missionary Society Collection, British Museum, London.

This carving, of superb quality, served as a funnel to feed liquid foods to certain persons, who for tapu reasons could not handle foods. Chiefs whose faces were swollen after tattooing sessions and who were under tapu would have found such an aid in taking food and drink a great comfort in time of need.

THE SPIRAL

75

MANY CARVED HOUSES have male and female images set on the underside of the porch section of the ridge-beam. Such pairs, whose sexual organs are sometimes joined, are said to represent Rangi the Sky-Father and Papa the Earth-Mother.

98 ◁

A ridge carving from the porch section of a small house. *Dimensions:* 43″ (109cm) × 12″ (30.5cm). *Collection:* Gisborne Museum, Gisborne.

The measurements of this carving are especially significant as they give an idea of the size of the house from which it came. In modern times it is hard to imagine an important house with a porch only forty-three inches wide, or a carved house generally proportioned to this small size, yet this old ridge-piece is firm evidence of the former existence of one such house, and suggests the former existence of inferior houses of small dimensions with important porch and frontal carvings, (it is unlikely that the former would exist without the latter).

99-100 ▷

Massive ridge carvings which were originally in the feet-to-feet position of the typical Rangi and Papa but have since been sawn into two parts. They are from the porch section of a house named Rangitihi which formerly stood at Taheke, Lake Rotoiti. By the workings of fate and the offerings of antique dealers both parts have found their way to Russia where they rest in the Leningrad Museum of Anthropology and Ethnology. The author has been obliged to use an old Dominion Museum glass negative which, through an act of curious prudery by person or persons unknown, has had the penis of the Rangi image (99) painted out. The sexual symbolism of Maori carving is both dignified and appropriate to the art, and it should not be messed about with in such an inane manner. Comments on this aspect of Maori art are given at some length in the Introduction.

101 ▽

The restored façade of Te Hau-ki-Turanga. A fully carved tribal meeting-house served a Maori community as guest-house, council-house, cultural centre and focal point of tribal mana. The Dominion Museum meeting-house named Te Hau-ki-Turanga ("the life-breath of Turanga", Turanga being the old Maori name for the Gisborne district) was built in 1842–43 at Manutuke by the Ngati Kaipoho and stood on the original site until it was taken to Wellington in 1867. The fascinating history of Te Hau-ki-Turanga, with the names of the ancestors represented by its carvings and its carvers, was published by the author in 1965. (See Bibliography.) The builder and "owner" of the house was the master-carver of the Gisborne school, Raharuhi Rukupo, whose portrait (102) stands on the left immediately inside the house. Te Hau-ki-Turanga was fitted into a ferro-concrete housing in the Maori Hall of the Dominion Museum when a new museum and national art gallery building was erected in 1935. Te Hau-ki-Turanga has inspired many houses, including Te Mana-o-Turanga (107–111), which stands at Manatuke near the original site of Te Hau-ki-Turanga; it has also served as the inspiration of a house carved by Pine Taiapa and his team at Whangara (79), and the Mormon Polynesian Cultural Centre house at Laie, Oahu, Hawaii, by Hone Taiapa OBE.

A portrait image, 44″ (111.7cm) high, representing Raharuhi Rukupo and believed to be a self-portrait (see the sketch, 10).

Raharuhi Rukupo was a chief of high rank who was also a master carver and a leader of the Turanga or Gisborne school of carving. He directed eighteen carvers in the production of the masterly panels and rafters of Te Hau-ki-Turanga. Raharuhi held firmly to Maori traditions until his death in 1873, and it is said of him that he was always strongly opposed to the inroads of the European settlers at Poverty Bay and to their Christian teaching. Apprenticed in the tradition of the stone adze and chisel, Raharuhi came to maturity as a carver at the time when iron and steel tools had replaced the old stone adze and chisel, although it is likely that he had had some experience with the old tools and had served apprentice-ship under a master who had learnt his art in the stone age.

Whatever his training, Raharuhi Rukupo was a master carver and Te Hau-ki-Turanga expresses his genius. This house is widely regarded as a masterwork and as the finest house to have survived from the 19th century. Fire and decay consumed dozens of good houses and it is a lucky thing for New Zealanders, Maori and Pakeha alike, that Te Hau-ki-Turanga is preserved into modern times and now encased in ferro-concrete housing. By the mid 1840s most carving areas were defunct, but the East Coast-Bay of Plenty region was notable as a survival area and for the persistence of carving tradition. The style of this house of Raharuhi Rukupo is bursting with the vitality and freedom brought about by steel tools and by western cultural ideas and technology. This, at first, brought a new and lavish form of meeting-house, then a decline in achievement as houses got progressively bigger.

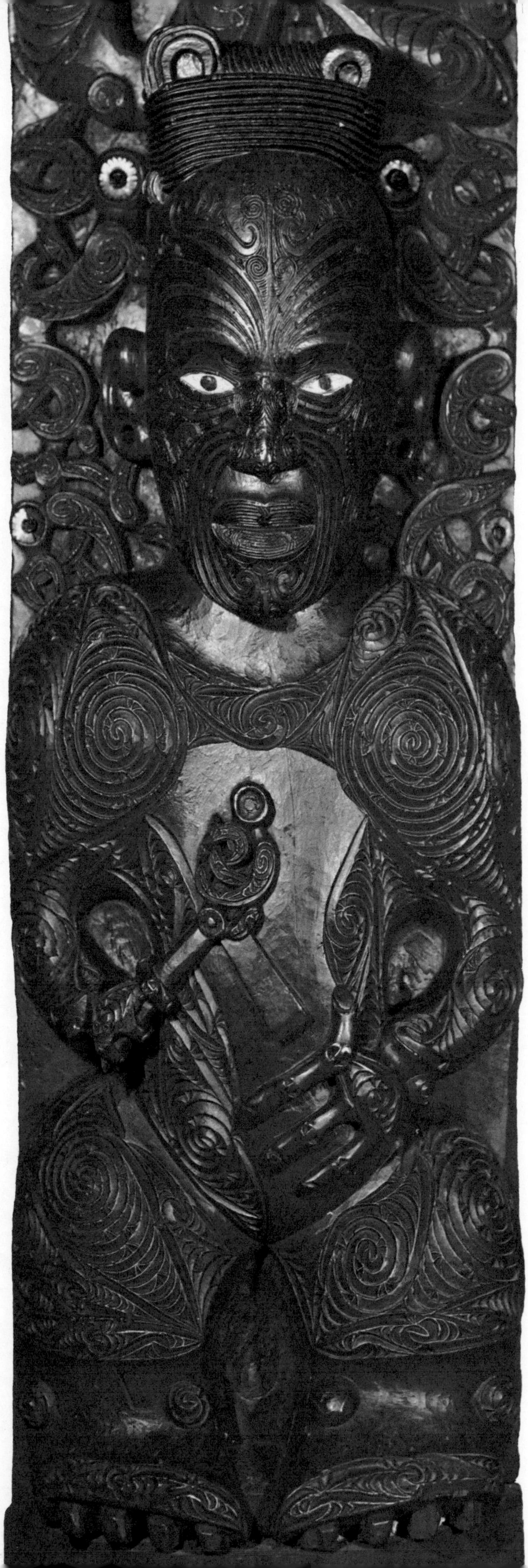

⇡ **103**
Interior panel (*poupou*), Te Hau-ki-Turanga (101), depicting a
fierce male ancestor with war club (*patu*) in hand and tongue
thrust out in defiance. The meeting-house was a central
structure in any village of standing. The ancestors represented
in the panels of a house served as a kind of book of tribal
history. Young and old alike regarded the images as material
vehicles used by ancestral spirits who took an active interest
in the affairs of their tribe. Because of the great admiration for
fighting men and their importance in tribal organisation,
ancestors are usually portrayed in war-dance postures.

⇨ **104**
Interior panel (*poupou*) representing an ancestress suckling a
child at her breast. The small figure set between the legs in
the position of a maternal delivery conveys the idea of tribal
continuity even when such "birth figures" are set between the
legs of male images.

105 ⬑
Interior view of a corner of Te Hau-ki-Turanga (101) showing the relationship of carvings, rafters, and the lattice panels (*tukutuku*). The main ancestral panels (*poupou*) in this house are surmounted by small relief images on the low ends of the rafters. The secondary images, called "sons" by one Maori, show a variety of surface adzing techniques. The rafters are magnificently decorated with painted patterns (*kowhaiwhai*).

106 ⬊
Panel image (*poupou*) in Te Hau-ki-Turanga (101) with the ancestral name KAHUTIA carved on its chest. Many of the lettered names on figures, in Te Hau-ki-Turanga and in other houses, appear to have a form derived from the Victorian typefaces used in the letterpress of missionary books such as hymnbooks and the Christian scriptures then available to the Maori. This ancestor and several others including Raharuhi Rukupo (102), hold a chiefly adze of authority (*toki-pu-tangata*) across the body (for a *toki-pu-tangata* see 196).

107 ⬧

108 ⬧

TRIBAL MEETING HOUSE TE MANA-O-TURANGA

T E MANA-O-TURANGA, also called Te Moana-nui-o-
Kiwa or Tauranganui-o-Kiwi, stands at Manutuke near the former site of Te-Hau-ki-Turanga
(101). In fact it is a legitimate descendant of the
Te-Hau-ki-Turanga or Gisborne school, but as the
house was built as late as 1883, about forty years
after Te Hau-ki-Turanga, it was more influenced by
western culture than by its illustrious predecessor.
Te Mana-o-Turanga has many delightful naturalistic
and painted sculptures which are foreign to traditional Maori wood carvings and which suggest the
figures of European folk art. Te Mana-o-Turanga
combines old and new styles in a remarkable and
forceful manner, and tells the stories of particular
tribal ancestors, wars, and adventures from the time
of Maui hauling up New Zealand to the time when
the house was built.

Photograph of Te Mana-o-Turanga as seen about the turn of
the century. This photograph may be compared with the
author's photograph (107) of the house taken in 1960, some
years after major restorations had considerably altered its
appearance. Unfortunately many fine New Zealand houses
have been indiscriminately repainted with modern red paints,
and thus much of the old quality has been lost. The façade of
Te Mana-o-Turanga depicts, in folk terms, the separation of
the sky parents Rangi and Papa, while a canoe containing
Maui with his reluctant brothers is seen with a whale which
represents the North Island (*Te Ika-roa-a-Maui*). The side
panels (*amo*), which support the frontal boards (*maihi*), are
slanted inwards in the manner of some early houses.

109 ⬧

Panels in the porch of Te Mana-o-Turanga as they stood about
1935 when the Wellington photographer W. Hall Raine made
this record. The older photograph (108) shows the house on
the ground, while this photograph shows how the panels
have been lifted by placement of a skirting base panel, which
was a way of getting the higher walls made fashionable by
modern living.

108

110 ◁

Porch panel (*poupou*) of Te Mana-o-Turanga (107). *Height:* 5′ 8″. (172.7cm)

The ancestor depicted has a manaia-headed fish set diagonally across its body, and the right hand is converted into a manaia with fingers projecting above the head. The style of the Te Mana-o-Turanga panels (109–111), carved in the 1880s, may be closely compared with those of Te Hau-ki-Turanga. The Te Mana-o-Turanga panels are greater in vertical height, and evidently cut from mill-supplied timber as the figures are of very low relief.

111 ▷

Porch panel (*poupou*) of Te Mana-o-Turanga (107). *Height:* 5′ 8″. (172.7cm)

Represented on this panel is Tutekohi, who lived early in the 17th century, with his dog and the gourd in which the dog's food was stored. The appearance of Tutekohi recalls the tale of the second big exodus of the Ngati Kahungunu folk from the Turanga district following contention which arose because of the disappearance of Tutekohi's dog. The dog vanished during a visit of one Rakaipaaka and his man, so Tutekohi put the man and his party under suspicion (we must recall that dogs were then regarded as delicious eating). The exchange of insults led to grievances and so to eventual bloodshed.

TRIBAL MEETING-HOUSE: TAMA-TE-KAPUA

112 ⇧

The ceremonial carved house (*whare-whakairo*) named Tama-te-Kapua stands at Ohinemutu, Rotorua.

Tama-te-Kapua was erected by the Ngati-Whakaue in 1878 at a time of revival of Maori custom (*tanga*). It was intended by the Arawa people as a token of reconciliation and friendship with the Waikato tribes whom they had opposed by fighting on the Pakeha side in the troubled times of the Maori Wars. Thus Tama-te-Kapua was offered as an inducement to have King Tawhiao visit Arawa territory, but this conciliatory invitation was of no avail at that time.

Tama-te-Kapua is one of the most famous of New Zealand houses. It has a large interior measuring 52' by 30' and was named after an earlier house which stood on Mokoia Island in Lake Rotorua. Tama-te-Kapua is the primal canoe ancestor of the Arawa people and the name honours his memory. The house is, in the esoteric sense, his body. Like other meeting-houses of 19th century date it has had restorations and reconstructions, namely in 1904 and about 1940. Some of the changes have made it more useful as a communal house, but less attractive as an artistic creation. Most of the carvings were freshly painted in refurbishment and were set above benches and at a much higher elevation than in the original structure (115). Most of the carvings appear to date from the 1870s and are of flattish or slightly rounded form. Many of the individual panels may be identified as particular ancestors by tribal memory of them, and in some instances the symbolism confirms contemporary identifications (104, 105).

⇩ 113

Interior panel (*poupou*), Tama-te-Kapua, Ohinemutu, Rotorua. *Height:* 5' 8". (172.7cm)

This panel is a good example of identification of the ancestor it represents by reference to a particular symbol. The flute (*putorino*) which is held vertically indicates it is Tutanekai who guided the beautiful and noble Hinemoa on her long night swim to her lover from the shore of Lake Rotorua to Tutanekai's island of Mokoia. The story of Hinemoa and Tutanekai is one of the most romantic of Maori legends.

◁114

Interior panel (*poupou*) of Tama-te-Kapua, Ohinemutu, Rotorua. *Height:* 5′ 8″. (172.7cm)

The design of this carving is typical of the highly involved work of Tama-te-Kapua panels which are formed by a large primary and surrounding manaia. Manaia, known in their local carved forms by the name of *toroa* (albatross or mollymawk) are of stylised birds with beaks that are sometimes exceptionally long. Two manaia seen on the body of this ancestor have elongated mandibles which reach to the ears in the conventional manner.

115▷

Interior panels of Tama-te-Kapua were originally set directly on the earth in typical Maori fashion as is seen in this photograph taken by the Burton brothers of Dunedin about 1880.

The figure represented on stilts in the central panel is either Tama-te-Kapua or his brother Whakaturia. In far Hawaiki these daring brothers deliberately committed sacrilege by raiding the sacred breadfruit tree of high priest Uenuku. They used stilts to avoid leaving footprints, but they were eventually caught in the act. Partly as a result of this outrage inter-group warfare broke out on the island. The faction of Tama-te-Kapua and Whakaturia were unsuccessful and by the grace of the stronger party and in accord with an old Polynesian custom of war, they were allowed to build canoes to go in search of new lands. Te Arawa was one of the canoes they built.

THE MODERN MEETING-HOUSE

Extant Maori carved houses (*whare-whakairo*) fall into two categories: those of central importance in the study of meeting-houses, such as Te Hau-ki-Turanga (101), Te Mana-o-Turanga (107) and Tama-te-Kapua (112); and other houses, of secondary status. The latter are of no less an importance to their Maori owners than the large impressive house, but to the student of Maori carving art they are of lesser value because of their late date and consequent distance in time from the earlier skills and carving traditions. Houses of the second class are typically modelled on the western building, with many windows and high doors, and in some instances these houses have attached kitchens and toilets, *noa* (common) additions that would have horrified the old-timer because of their tapu-destroying qualities. Steel-tool houses made about a hundred years ago tended to use split tree slabs or heavy pit-sawn timbers for panel work. Narrow flat boards of the late period engendered high walls. Commercially sawn boards, power tools, and corrugated iron had a profound influence on the form of the finished house.

116 ⇧
This small meeting-house, named Te Ngatau, opened in 1894, is typical of dozens of local houses which cannot rank with Te Hau-ki-Turanga and the larger 19th century houses as objects of study, yet they are interesting and perform a good community service to their owners.

Mr W. J. Phillipps, who served for many years on the staff of the Dominion Museum, is seen seated on the *paepae* during his visit to this house. Over many years during his working life and in retirement until his death in 1967 Mr Phillipps continued to collect data and write on Maori carving and other aspects of Maori life. He published extensively on Maori meeting-houses and foodstores, and his useful work will assist students of Maori architecture for many generations to come, particularly because no house was too modest or too small for his attentive noting. Also, he was not prone to that criticism of quality of a work that an art historian must make in his selection and judgements when the aesthetics of sculpture are involved. Mr Phillipps was impersonal in his work, and this is one of its most valuable aspects.

117 ⇨
A late 19th century house panel in the collection of the American Museum of Natural History, New York, USA.

The panel depicts the demigod Maui hauling to the surface a fish which here symbolises the North Island of New Zealand which is traditionally known as the Fish of Maui—*Te Ika-a-Maui*, or *Te Ika-roa-a-Maui*—the Long Fish of Maui. The carving style is Arawa, Bay of Plenty.

118 ⇨
A modern rendering in form of western mermaid of an old carving motif depicting a sea-monster called *marakihau* (50, 52, 53). This use of a European mythical creature to serve the purpose of a fabulous Maori sea monster, and the adaptations of Western realism in carving art represents a kind of folk style and is delightful, but decadent as compared with the old austere styles of early times. This panel is in an East Coast house.

93

HOUSE DOOR LINTELS

Door lintels (*pare* or *korupe*) of diverse sizes, regions, styles, and ages, have been preserved in good numbers in the museums of New Zealand, America, Britain and continental Europe. The lintel was a vital carving in the traditional ceremonial carved house and of ritualistic importance because it neutralised harmful tapu as a person entered or left a house. Specimens have survived in large numbers and they provide tangible evidence of the existence of many houses lost without trace.

Why have so many *pare* survived when the other carvings of houses have been lost for ever? The logical probabilities are as follows: door lintels were attractive to curio or souvenir hunters from the time of Captain Cook onwards; they could be readily detached with or without the owners' permission; when tribal territory was threatened Maori tribes sometimes detached the most important carvings for concealment in swamp or cave; and the magical power of *pare* must have placed them high for mana. There is also significance in the view that there were few fully carved houses in Prehistoric times although the superior house with frontal mask (*koruru*), carved bargeboards (*maihi*) and doorway (including pare), were relatively common.

119 ⬑

A door lintel (*pare*) composed of three outward-facing images with manaia "hands" raised to the head, and numerous intermediate manaia elaborating the general design. The *pare* is of Bay of Plenty style. *Dimensions:* 4'2″ × 1'7″ (127.1cm × 48.8cm). *Collection:* Dominion Museum, Wellington.

Pare in general provide a remarkable range of manaia interspersed tiki figures. Manaia commonly form the outer ends of the lintels (120, 123, 126), and supplementary spirals are used in *pare* compositions.

122 ⇨

Door lintels (*pare*), of Bay of Plenty style composed of three ancestral images with their hands converted into manaia heads, and intermediate massive interlocking spirals. *Dimensions:* 50″ (127cm) × 16″ (41cm). *Collection:* Bernice P. Bishop Museum, Honolulu, Hawaii. This *pare* was purchased in the Eric Craig Collection of Maori carving.

120 ⇧

Door lintels (*pare*) with central human figure and involved manaia. *Dimensions:* 41½" (105cm) × 13¾" (35cm). *Collection:* National Museum of Ireland, Dublin.

This *pare* was accepted into the Museum collection in 1886 but was probably collected in New Zealand well before that date.

121 ⇩

Door lintel (*pare*) with elongated manaia reaching to the head of a central tiki image. *Dimensions:* 41" (104cm) × 10" (25cm). *Collection:* The Montreal Museum of Fine Arts, Canada.

Formerly in the H. G. Beasely Collection, Cranmore Museum, this *pare* was taken to England early in the 19th century. Some of the manaia are of distinctly birdlike form.

123 ⇧

This door lintel (*pare*) was unearthed from Hauraki Plains at Papetonga in 1919. *Dimensions: Width:* 7'7". (233.8cm) *Height:* 2'6" (76.2cm). *Collection:* Auckland Institute and Museum, Auckland.

It is of vigorous northern style, and is one of the most masterly examples of Maori carving remaining in modern times. The curvilinear elements are set around the forward-facing images, which have whole paua shells inset as eyes, while the feet are webbed like the feet of waterbirds. The spirals appear derived from the interlocking of manaia beaks. The manaia heads are rendered in extremely simple terms but the outward-turned manaia grasping "snake" on the sides of the *pare* are complete "bird-men" of a sophisticated kind.

124 ⇩

Door lintel (*pare*) found in 1959 at Waitara in the side of a drainage ditch about five feet below ground level. A boy named Shaun Ainsworth had gone to a drainage ditch in search of a suitable place to release a pet frog that had grown unhappy in captivity when he saw this carving projecting from the mud. *Dimensions:* 5'11" (180cm) × 1'9" (53cm). *Collection:* Taranaki Museum, New Plymouth.

The carving style is classic Taranaki style and typical of a number that have been found, haphazardly, by local people (compare 156). In placing this carving with lintels the author records his opinion that it is conceivably a baseboard from the front of a storehouse of the type seen in the Heaphy sketch (157).

125 ⇪
Upper part of a door lintel (*pare*) of East Coast type which is related in general characteristics to the lintel illustrated below (126). This beautiful fragment is in the collection of the Anthropological Museum, Marischael College, University of Aberdeen, Scotland.

126 ⇩
Door lintel (*pare*) of East Coast style. *Dimensions:* 38½″ (98cm) × 2′6″ (76cm). Presented to the British Museum, London, by Sir George Grey in the year 1854.

The out-turned manaia, which grapple with the manaia-headed "snake", stand on large manaia heads which relate in turn to the stylisation of the whale head of the Te Kaha barge-board (55–57) and other foodstore "whales".

Certain carvings are directly associated with the bones of the dead while others are merely dedicated to the memory of the dead. Memorial carvings may commemorate the place of death of a notable person, or his memory, or an event related to his death such as the stopping place of his corpse en route to the burial. In pre-European times the place of burial was not marked as there was a well-based fear that enemies of the deceased would happily desecrate the bones by converting them into fish-hooks, flutes, and other useful objects. This was an extreme insult and humiliation to the dead man and to his living relations.

127 ◁

A sacred marker (*pou-rahui*) set up at Waitahanui pa to help define a tapu line across Lake Taupo ending at Pukawa, where a second post was placed. The purpose of the posts was to mark a taboo area on Lake Taupo after the death of Heuheu Tukino II and many members of the Tuwharetoa tribe who had died in a terrible landslide which overwhelmed the village of Te Rapa in 1846. The *pou-rahui* was photographed *in situ* in 1904 by M. McDonald and was later carried to the Auckland Institute and Museum, where it now stands in the Maori Hall.

128 ▷

A lithograph of a carved tomb entitled: "Monument to Te Whero's Daughter at Raroera Pah." From the album *The New Zealanders Illustrated* by George French Angas, first published in London, 1846. According to Angas the corpse was placed in this elaborate tomb until a time when the flesh was decayed and the bones ready for uplifting and final "bone" burial. This practice of second burial was a standard pre-Christian Maori custom when the body of a person of rank was concerned. This tomb measured about 12' to 14' high and was executed by one man, his only instrument being "an old bayonet".

Bone-chests (*waka-tupapaku* or *atamiro*) commonly termed "burial chests", served to contain the bones of chiefs of high tribal status. They were formed by hollowing the back of a specially made image and constructing a rear door which was sometimes hinged. Considerable numbers of chests have been located in caves in the Auckland district, and isolated boxes have been found as far south as Horowhenua in the Wellington district, and from Ruapuke Island in Foveaux Strait at the bottom of the South Island. The Ruapuke box, which is in the Otago Museum, has the body of a bird and the head of a man.

When a person of rank died his body was either buried, placed in a cave, or raised on a platform and preferably in a concealed place. After two years the bones were gathered, scraped, then coated with red ochre with all due ceremony. They were then by one means or another given a second and final "burial". Occasionally the skull alone was uplifted (see the skull boxes 13, 130). Bone chests appear to have originated from the use of burial canoes. Their name supports this idea *waka,* a canoe and *tupapaku,* a corpse, but the strongest evidence of canoe relationship is in the form of these chests: many have a distinct keel-like ridge running down the centre of the body and when seen in profile the shape resembles a canoe. This canoe-like chest contained the bones of a chief whose spirit was believed to travel back over the myriad miles of sea to the far Hawaiki homeland.

⇧**129**
A massive bone-chest (*waka-tupapaku*) formed as a female image. *Height:* 46½″ (118cm). *Collection:* Dominion Museum, Wellington.

This magnificent prehistoric specimen has retained areas of the original red ochre (*kokowai*) traditionally painted on bone-chests but almost always weathered off. A manaia, of a type associated with northern bone-chests, reaches up to the head of the image in the manner of manaia behaviour well known to Classic carving.

130 ⇩
Slab from a skull box of a type known from two complete specimens, one in the Otago and the other in the Canterbury Museum. *Dimensions:* 18″ (46cm) × 10½″ (27cm). *Collection:* Otago Museum, Dunedin.

The design includes full mask and a profile head known as the *ngututa*. This head should not be confused with the manaia, from which it differs in important respects (see page 63).

▷ **131-132**

Two views of a bone-chest (*waka-tupapaku*) believed to have been collected by a Captain A. J. Higgins about the middle of the 19th century. *Height:* 36½″ (93cm). *Collection:* British Museum, London.

The damaged side and base are typical of the type of decay found on many bone-chests. Smaller chests frequently have peg bases which allow them to stand on the floor of a cave, and the peg was quite naturally the first part of the box to rot away. When the box fell the side it fell on then decayed, a sequence of events that in some instances left only one side of the box or merely tantalising fragments on the floor of the cave.

▷ **133**

Bone-chest (*waka-tupapaku*) from Raglan, Auckland. *Height:* 39″ (99cm). *Collection:* Dominion Museum, Wellington.

The head compares in style with the heads of the Hauraki lintel images (123), and it is also adapted to receive whole small paua-shell eyes. In this case the shell eyes have been lost from the chest, but the sockets are of the kind made to hold whole shells. A "keel ridge" runs up the centre of the body.

Godsticks, termed *tiki-wananga* or *whakapakoko rakau* in New Zealand, have related forms in the tropical central islands of Polynesia, and exact counterparts to the Maori godsticks are found in Hawaiian collections. The New Zealand godsticks were used by priests, who either thrust them into the ground or held them in the hand, then called on the god to inhabit them. Their form comprises a mask on a shaft which is normally pointed, or a whole image on a peg (142). Godsticks with additional bodily features such as upper limbs (136) and double heads (139, 24) are rare in New Zealand. In fact, godsticks generally are among the rarest of Maori artifacts, although some twenty-seven were searched out and published by the author (see Bibliography, Barrow 1959, 1961.).

Godsticks were in no sense worshipped. They merely served as material vehicles for the gods or spirits they were said to represent, and their identity appears to have been designated by the priest who used the image and not because of particular features of the godstick. Those identified as individual gods were so named by Maoris for missionary collectors. The Rev Richard Taylor conveniently pencilled the name on the specimen. In use, a godstick was not considered effective until it was painted with red ochre (*kokowai*), bound with flax fibre cord, and dressed with feathers which were either thrust into or bound into the lashing. The mystical power of cordage, of red clay and red feathers, was basic to the material symbolism of Polynesian religion. Almost all the recovered godsticks relate to the Wanganui and Taranaki regions although one (24–25) has been found in the South Island.

135 ⇨
Godstick (*tiki-wananga*) with bound shaft. *Height:* 12″ (30.5 cm). *Collection:* Pitt Rivers Museum, Oxford, England. Collected by the Rev Richard Taylor, presumably in the Wanganui district, about mid-19th century.

134 ⇧
Godsticks (*tiki-wananga*) representing Hukere, a deity believed to have been local to the Wanganui district. Head detail of 136 (see caption for additional data). The style of the head appears to be of archaic Polynesian type related to certain Hawaiian image forms.

136 ⇨
Godstick (*tiki-wananga*) representing Hukere (for head detail see 134). *Height:* 14⅜″ (36.5cm). *Collection:* Cambridge University Museum of Archaeology and Ethnology, Cambridge, England. Collected by the Rev Richard Taylor, presumably in the Wanganui district, about mid-19th century.

137 ⇨
Godstick (*tiki-wananga*) representing Kahukura, a war god of Rarotonga associated with the Aotea and Takitimu canoes. *Height:* 14½″ (37cm). *Collection:* University Museum of Archaeology and Ethnology, Cambridge, England. Collected by the Rev Richard Taylor, presumably in the Wanganui district, about mid-19th century.

135   136   137

Godstick (*tiki-wananga*) said to represent Rongo, collected at Waimate (Taranaki) about 1840 with godsticks (138–139) and (141). *Height:* 12⅜″ (31.5cm). *Collection:* Auckland Institute and Museum, Auckland.

138-139 ⇧ ⇧
Front and side views of a godstick (*tiki-wananga*) recorded as representing Tangaroa (or Turanga). It was collected with godsticks (140) and (141) at Waimate, Taranaki, about 1840, by William Hough, a Wesleyan catechist stationed at Waimate. *Height:* 12¼″ (31cm). The double-headed image is an old Oceanic artistic device also seen in the Otago godstick (24–25). *Collection:* Auckland Institute and Museum, Auckland.

⇧**141**
Godstick (*tiki-wananga*) with vestigial coxcomb crest, and reported as representing the war god Maru. Collected at Waimate (Taranaki) about 1840 with godsticks (138–139) and (140). *Height:* 9⅝″ (24.5cm). *Collection:* Auckland Institute and Museum, Auckland.

⇨**142**

A rare godstick (*tiki-wananga*) with full image mounted on a stout peg. *Overall height:* 14″ (35.5cm); *height of image:* 10¾″ (27.5cm). Holes above the outer part of the eyes served as tie-points for the feather bundles which were so important in the dressing of a god.

This fine specimen was purchased in open auction at Sotheby's of London by Mr K. A. Webster. Its provenience is unknown, but considering the basis of style as an index of origin, it probably came from the East Coast district. The three projections above the head appear to be the remains of a comb and not of a crest of the coxcomb type with which it might be confused (as seen for example, in the godstick 141).

STOCKADE IMAGES

VILLAGES with defensive palisading were set on flatland or on terraced hill sites and were formed throughout the North Island and in many parts of the South Island in Classic Maori times. The introduction of the musket and steel axe rendered Classic fortifications obsolete, for obvious reasons. The stockade villages were deserted after tribes who were favourably placed to trade for muskets early in the 19th century made use of their advantage and turned to scourge neighbours who were still armed with stone and wooden weapons and were confident in the effectiveness of wooden stockades. Before the musket devastation, villages of any status or strategic importance had defiant images carved on the highest posts in the defensive palisades. These stockade images, which are now found cut from their base posts, served to boost the morale of those within the compounds. They also serve to express contempt for attacking forces and, as many represented the ancestral spirits of the tribe, they were thought to aid in the defence of a village.

143 ⬂

This painting of a typical East Coast fortified hill village (*pa*) was composed by Marcus King in 1949 from a model in the Dominion Museum. Villages were either lightly defended or elaborately fortified. Stockade images, carved gateways, and the carved houses and storehouses of a prosperous community may be seen in this painting.

144 ⬀

Some villages possessed massive wooden gateways and commemorative posts. This carving, now in the collection of the Auckland Museum, was cut from either a large post or a gateway. Its present height is 6′8″, width 4′8″. Original height, 15′. According to Augustus Hamilton's classic volume, *The Art Workmanship of the Maori Race in New Zealand* (1896), this carving came from Te Ngae on the shore of Lake Rotorua, and the main figure represents a chief of the Ngati-Whakaue called Pukaki. The small figures set on the torso relate to the series of figures in sexual embrace found on foodstore façades (154–155), and more rarely elsewhere (similar pairs sometimes appear on bowls, canoe prows, house panels and house posts).

145

Tu Kaitote Pa on the Waikato River as seen by George French Angas early in the 19th century, lithographed for *The New Zealanders Illustrated*, London, 1846. Angas describes this pa as "the principal abode of the celebrated chief Te Werowero, who is head of all the Waikato Tribes". The heavy knobbed stockade posts seen on the right probably derive from highly conventionalised human images.

146

Many stockades incorporating human images were found on flat land on or near lake shores. This view of Waitahanui pa on the shores of Lake Taupo was also sketched by George French Angas for his album of lithographs entitled *The New Zealanders Illustrated*, London, 1846. Angas drew this scene by stealth, as the pa was then tabooed by Te Heuheu who had specifically forbidden Angas to draw sacred objects while travelling in his territory.

147-148

foot of Te Uhi hill, Wairoa. It was deposited by its owner, Mrs Dorrie Chapman, with the Wairoa Public Library to protect it from the weather. The wood from which it was made had certain large knots which give the figure its particular strength and character, and without those it is unlikely that it could have survived to the present day.

A stockade post image said to represent Kawiti, an important Stone-age chief of the Ngati-Kurupakiaka *hapu. Height:* 84″. (213.2cm) The base post has been cut off.

Until 1964 this fine figure, which has exceptional sculptural vigour, stood at the Maori settlement at the

111

149 ◁

An image cut from a palisade post. *Height of figure: 67"* (170.2cm) *Collection:* Hawke's Bay Museum, Napier.

This ancestral tiki, which has erect penis and holds a war club in hand, is depicted in haka posture. The staring expression defied the would-be attackers of a village and, in Maori belief, it added the power of magic to village defence. The exact provenience of this figure is unknown but it probably is from an East Coast pa.

⇩ **150**

An image of the stockade type which has been cut from its base post. *Height:* 50¾″ (129cm). *Collection:* National Museum of Denmark, Copenhagen.

Museum records indicate that this image came from Te Awamutu before 1896 (the year of its accession in Copenhagen). The style is that of the Bay of Plenty while the sculptural form may be compared with 144. The heavily-weathered surfaces, seen in so many stockade figures, enhance rather than detract from the beauty of this carving.

113

151-152 ⇧ ⇧

Two aspects of a small image which has one hand upraised to the mouth. *Height:* 12″ (30cm). *Collection:* Otago Museum, Dunedin. This small figure was cut from a house gatepost at a Maori settlement (Kaianga) in Whetu Gorge.

The figure appears in Hamilton's *Maori Art* (1896) with a note that it formerly belonged to Kereopa who starred in the blood-drinking and eye-swallowing ritual at Opotiki after the murder of the Rev Carl Sylvius Volkner in 1865. The carving was presented to the Otago Museum by Lady Chapman. It has an inscription on the back, in the hand of Sir Frederick Chapman (1849–1936), which confirms it was from a gatepost of the house of Kereopa with this added information: "It was cut off the post with a pocket knife saw by Mr Hoyte an artist who brought it away in a knapsack and ultimately gave it to me at Dunedin about 1876."

STOREHOUSE CARVINGS

Storehouses (*pataka*) ranked with superior carved houses as the most important structures in a village. The best available carving talent was lavished on them and their carvings were prized by the community. Foodstores have exterior carvings on the façade and in the shallow porch, but, in contrast to the exterior. *Pataka* were used as foodstores but had a variety of other uses, including that of safeguarding rare and valued possessions. They kept foods away from the ravages of rats and from pollution by unauthorised hands. Precious things were best stored out of common touch. As structures, *pataka* differed in size and type. Taboos relating to the food and possessions of high-ranking members of the community were scrupulously maintained with the held of these buildings.

⌂ **153**
A watercolour sketch of storehouses (*pataka*) by Augustus Earle, an English artist who went to New Zealand in 1827 (see also the Earle sketch 204). Earle established his headquarters at Kororareka (Russell), in the Bay of Islands. A painting of a Wanganui village (167) with storehouses, by J. A. Gilfillan, illustrates by contrast the great changes wrought in Maori village life within the two decades represented at first and last by these pictures.

154 ⇦

A vertical panel, one of a pair supporting the left bargeboard (*maihi*) of the Arawa storehouse named Puawai-o-te-Arawa (Flower of the Arawa). As it was formerly the property of Te Pohika Taranui (Major Fox), it is generally called the "Fox Pataka". Now re-erected in the Maori Hall of Auckland Museum, this storehouse originally stood where it was built at Maketu in the Bay of Plenty about 1860 by Pokiha Haranui. Pokiha Haranui, younger brother of Waata Haranui who had built the house named Rangatiki at Whakarewarewa, felt the need to establish his own mana so he decided to construct this outsize *pataka*. Puawai-o-te-Arawa, which measures 35' by 20', is the largest storehouse in existence and probably the largest ever made in New Zealand. The panel subject of male (*right*) and female (*left*) in sexual embrace is found on storehouse façades (153, 155, 204) and doorways (163), and elsewhere in Maori carving (see note to 144). This sexual symbolism is not clearly understood although it probably expresses the desire of the tribe to survive through increasing fertility and abundance. Erotic symbolism is prevalent in Maori wood sculpture; however, it is never a pornographic art.

155 ⇨

This superb foodstore fragment relates very closely to those seen on the Earle *pataka* (153), and is directly related to other foodstore panels of same subject (154). The facial styles of the images, male (*right*) and female (*left*), suggest it has a Bay of Plenty provenience, however the actual history has been lost. K. A. Webster *Collection*.

This little masterwork, measuring only 13¾" (35cm) × 7½" (19cm), probably originated in the late 18th century. Unfortunately it has been ruthlessly censored by some misguided prude who sawed both figures through at the waist thus removing the "offending" lower half.

116

156 ◁

A storehouse (*pataka*) façade board (*epa*), recovered in 1958 from a swamp at Waitara, Taranaki. (Compare the similar Waitara *epa*, 124). *Dimensions:* 39″ (99cm) × 9½″ (24cm). *Collection:* Taranaki Museum, New Plymouth.

This panel and several others found in the Waitara swamps are probably of a related group and in some cases appear to come from the same structure. In the early 19th century a section of the Ati-Awa people occupied the Manukorihi pa, and it is likely that on the advance of musket-armed northern enemies these valuable carvings were detached by the local people and concealed in nearby swampy hollows. Attempts systematically to recover lost carvings have so far been unsuccessful. The best Waitara swamp recoveries have been by chance. They provide us with unsurpassed examples of the vigorous Taranaki style as it existed in the opening decades of the 19th century before its sudden demise under the devastating impact of western civilisation.

157 ◁

An 1840s sketch by Charles Heaphy of a Taranaki storehouse shown with Mount Egmont in the background. Heaphy came to New Zealand in the ship *Tory* in August 1839 as official draftsman of the New Zealand Company, for whom he visited Taranaki on survey duty in 1840. The style of the carvings on this complete *pataka* compare with 156, and the so-called lintel, 124. *Collection:* Alexander Turnbull Library, Wellington.

118

Provision House;

Otumatua Pah, Cape Egmont.

158 ⇩
A storehouse (*pataka*) central in a lithographic plate illustrating various storehouses in *The New Zealanders Illustrated*, London, 1846. The artist George French Angas sketched this *pataka* at Te Rapa on the shores of Lake Taupo. He says that the main use of storehouse structures was to give protection of food specially put aside for chiefs, and "apart from that eaten by women and slaves".

159 ⇧
View into the porch of a storehouse (*pataka*) from Lake
Rotoiti now in the National Museum of Denmark, Copenhagen, acquired in 1926. The figures on right and left panels
represent a particular spidery image style known from other
Bay of Plenty storehouses. Two manaia bite into the head of
the doorway images. The zigzag "water" pattern, generally
known by the Maori term *tara-tara-a-kai*, is usually restricted
to storehouses (for examples refer to 57, 65, 160), but it is
occasionally found on a few stockade images (147–148),
canoe "*tohunga*" thwarts, paddles, and bailers.

160 ⇧
A detail of the side of the "Fox *Pataka*" named Puawaı-o-te-Arawa (Flower of the Arawa) which was built at Maketu about 1860 by Pokiha Haranui (for additional history see the caption to the frontal panel (154) from the same storehouse). *Collection:* Auckland Institute and Museum, Auckland.

The earliest *pataka* were normally very small in size therefore the side walls of the oldest collected are often single slabs as formerly illustrated (64, 65). This Maketu storehouse measures about 35′ along each wall, so the craftsmen were obliged to form each wall by vertical panels lashed together in the manner of storehouse frontal boards (*epa*). This is one of the many interesting adaptations in Historic times. Manaia and tiki are placed in alternate position in the traditional manner (64, 65), but wall height is gained by the device of placing a mask under each unit of the design. An upper board fringes the overlapping and decorated eaves in a further innovation.

161 ⇧
Gable peak figure (*tekoteko*) from either a foodstore or small house. *Height:* 25½″ (65cm). *Collection:* British Museum, London.

This carving, which is composed of a tiki standing on a downward-facing mask, is covered with dull red paint while the incised facial tattoo (*moko*) of the upper image is traced over with black paint. Gable peak figures, and the masks on which they sometimes stand, are best viewed from below at an angle of about forty-five degrees. Interior house carvings are best viewed from a seated position on the floor. Thus there is a subtle perspective in Maori wood sculpture which is not yet widely appreciated. Maori craftsmen were well aware of the optical requirements of space and form in architecture, and followed certain principles in a tradition of profound craftsmanship.

122

162 ⇧
A door slab (*kuwaha*), from a storehouse, rebated, or slotted at the top to carry a ridge beam. *Dimensions:* 72″ (183cm) 28″ (71cm). *Collection:* The Manchester Museum, Manchester, England.

The style is that of the Arawa, Bay of Plenty. It compares well with (159). This storehouse doorway was purchased from an Auckland dealer, Eric Craig, about 1900, who sold a set of storehouse pieces as separate items to the Dominion Museum, the Otago Museum, and the Manchester Museum. Most of the façade of this storehouse is now assembled at the Dominion Museum, but this doorway remains in England. The remarkable story of these carvings is told in part by Mr Frank Willett of the Manchester Museum (see Bibliography).

⇧**163**
A door slab (*kuwaha*) from a storehouse of Bay of Plenty style. *Dimensions:* 54″ (137cm) × 28″ (71cm). *Collection:* Canterbury Museum, Christchurch.

The top is rebated to accommodate a ridge beam (compare 162). Its central subject is embracing male (*left*) and female (*right*) figures. This carving was formerly in the possession of the Auckland dealer Eric Craig.

Shark-tooth implements of various forms were used in several island groups of the Pacific, notably as weapons in the Gilbert and Hawaiian Islands. Maori shark-tooth knives are small yet of elaborate design, typically based on the manaia form. The name used for these knives is generally *maripi* but there are other names including *mira tuatini* (from *tuatina*, the species of shark favoured for teeth). There is a temptation to class these artifacts as weapons of war yet they are essentially saw-like knives intended for cutting by a slow pull toward the user. The suggestion that they are human flesh cutters is reasonable, but they may also have served as useful slicers in cutting any flesh, for example from sea mammals or large birds. It seems probable they were implements of cannibalism.

164 ◁

Shark-tooth knife (*maripi*) presented by Sir George Grey to the British Museum, London, in 1854. *Dimensions:* 9½″ (24cm) × 3¼″ (8.3cm). This knife has seven shark teeth set in a groove which holds them firm without aid of lashing. Paua shell is inlaid as eyes in the head of the manaia which grasps a "snake" (see the lintel terminations 71, 120, 123). A secondary manaia head is located at the back of the principal manaia.

165

Shark-tooth cutter with single tooth. *Dimensions overall:* 6¾″ (17.2cm), head, 1⅞″ (4.6cm). *Collection:* British Museum, London.

The handle of this cutter is surface decorated. A tooth from a blue shark (*mango-pounamu*) known to science as *Prionace glauca*, is attached by a two-ply twist which passes through holes made in both tooth and handle. Paua insets are placed in both eyes.

↶ 166
Shark-tooth knife (*maripi*) believed to have been collected on Cook's voyages, was presented to the Hunterian Museum, Glasgow University, Scotland, by a Captain King. The quality of the specimen, and the fact that several similar knives were collected by Cook and his men, reinforces the probability. *Length:* 8⅞″ (22.5cm).

The vertical row of drilled shark-teeth are set in a slot then lashed to the manaia-form handle. The hole at the base immediately above the pommel is drilled to receive a wrist thong (as seen intact in 164).

DOMESTIC CARVINGS

The everyday life of the Maori required a large number of carved objects of many uses. Many things served as ordinary household equipment while some objects were needed in the vital activities of fowling, fishing and food storage.

167 ⇧
This is a typical domestic scene in a village (*kainga*) of the early 19th century. The artist, John Alexander Gilfillan of Scotland, settled in the Wanganui district in 1841 where he followed pioneer farming but sketched as a hobby. The village represented here is on the banks of the Wanganui River and it was lithographed from a painting now lost. A carved house and storehouses of several types are included in the picture.

⇩ **168**
A dish with handle formed by an image. *Length overall:* 8¾″ (22cm). *Collection:* British Museum in 1870. The image style suggests a Taranaki provenience for this unusual small bowl.

126

169 ⇧
Food bowl (*kumete*) of animal form, presumably that of a pig, with head stylised as manaia. *Length:* 39¾″ (101cm). *Collection:* Cambridge University Museum of Archaeology and Ethnology.

The body of the bowl, which has traces of red ochre paint (*kokowai*) on it, is decorated with large spirals.

⇨ **170**
Spoon or scoop. *Length:* 12⅝″ (32cm). K.A. Webster *Collection*.

Traces of red paint, of *kokowai* type, suggest this artifact may have been used as an ochre scoop, but it may have been used in feeding highly tapu persons. The former use seems more probable.

⇧ **171-172** (view of end mask) ⇧
Carved perch. *Overall length* 9¾″ (25cm). *Collection:* Rijiksmuseum voor Volkenkunde, Leiden, Holland. Acquired by the Museum in 1883.

Carvings of this kind are usually described as "objects of unknown use", however their identification as bird perches of a ritualistic kind, for use in fowling at certain times, seems sufficiently reliable to allow the presentation of an example here. However this identification is tentative and not final.

173 ◁
A step (*teka*) of a digging-stick (*ko*). *Length:* 7⅝″ (19.4cm). K. A. Webster *Collection*.

Steps of this type are generally known as "foot-rests" and they were lashed at right angles to the lower end of the blade of a digging-stick. Their purpose was to enable the user to get a better downward thrust into the earth.

174 ⇨
Net-float (*poito*) of human form. *Dimensions:* 15¾″ (40cm) × 6¼″ (16cm). *Collection:* Dominion Museum, Wellington.

The hole at the crown of the image served as the tie-point where it was attached to a net.

128

129

CANOE CARVINGS

◁175
A war canoe with sail, as seen off Cape Egmont by the artist George French Angas. From a lithograph in *The New Zealanders Illustrated*, London, 1846.

◁176
A prow, from a small canoe of a type probably used as a burial canoe. *Dimensions:* 24⅝″ (60cm) × 10⅝″ (27cm) × 9″ (23cm). *Collection:* Bernice P. Bishop Museum, Honolulu, Hawaii.

Recorded as having come from the Rotorua Lake region, it is a singular miniature prow of a size consistent with a number of prows and sternposts. These are probably best interpreted by comparison with the prow and sternposts of the small Webster canoe (183). The caption to the latter is also relevant to this prow.

177 △
Detail of a war canoe prow (*tau-ihu*) showing the figurehead figure with winglike arms. *Total dimensions of prow:* 58″ (147 cm) × 28″ (71cm). *Collection:* Taranaki Museum, New Plymouth. An enlargement of the spiral detail on this prow appears as 96.

The canoe from which this prow was removed is said to have reached Taranaki in 1849 with Ati-Awa Maori returning from Waikanae.

131

178 ⊹
Canoe prow (*tau-ihu*), of a distinctive Taranaki style. *Dimensions:* 36″ (91cm) × 15″ (38cm). *Collection:* Taranaki Museum, New Plymouth.

This prow combines an arrangement of design elements of the classic war canoe prow, namely: forward-facing "figurehead" image—spiral—central figure—spiral—and aft-facing figure. An extreme version of this formula is seen in the prow from Mokau, North Taranaki (76, and line analysis 77) in which manaia "tails" form simple interlocking spirals.

179 ⇨
Detail of a canoe paddle showing images placed back-to-back and joined by intertwined limbs. The carving style is typical of the Taranaki region. *Collection:* British Museum, London.

⇨ **180**

A war canoe sternpost (*tau-rapa*) of Classic type as seen on the canoes in the Angas lithograph (175) and the Robley water-colour (191). *Length:* 5′8¼″ (173.3cm). *Width:* 1′1″ (33cm). *Collection:* Auckland Institute and Museum, Auckland.

Fully to appreciate this, or any other canoe sternpost, it is best to envisage it in relation to the whole canoe with its graceful lines. Prow and sternpost are really one, as they are connected in the general design by the topstrakes of the hull. The upward sweep of the sternpost is comprised of two great ribs which in fact form the backbone of the sternpost and provide the necessary structural strength to support the surrounding spirals and small manaia. In the Classic design, as seen here, the "ribs" are grasped at the top by a biting manaia while the squared top is formed by an abstract full-face crowned by "fingers". Connecting "chocks" in the general structure are strengtheners and are not an integral part of the design. A good illustration of this difference may be seen in the design analysis of the Taranaki prow (77) when viewed in comparison with the whole prow as seen in the photograph (76).

133

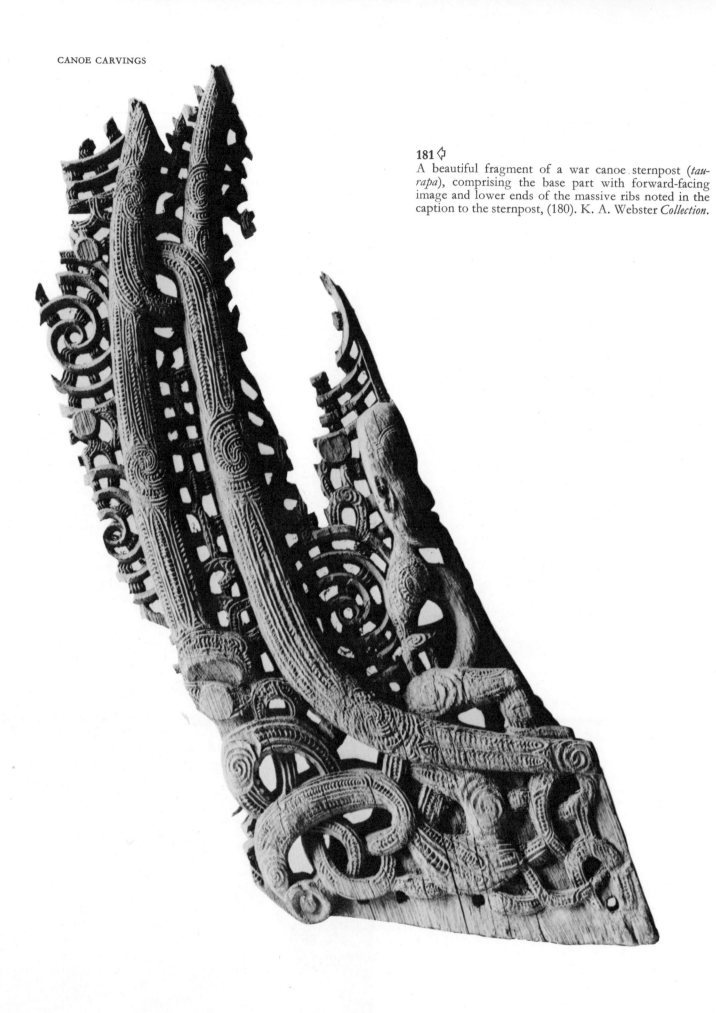

181 ⇦
A beautiful fragment of a war canoe sternpost (*tau-rapa*), comprising the base part with forward-facing image and lower ends of the massive ribs noted in the caption to the sternpost, (180). K. A. Webster *Collection*.

182 ◁
Sternpost (*tau-rapa*) of a small canoe. *Height:* 2'2" (66cm). W. O. Oldman *Collection,* Dominion Museum, Wellington. This sternpiece belonged to a small canoe of the type seen below (183).

↶**183**

This magnificent small canoe 16' 6" in length with decorated top-strakes and hull, (see manaia detail 69) has been described as a "model" canoe. Formerly K. A. Webster Collection but acquired in 1968 by Dr Peter Ludwig of Aachen who deposited it in the Cologne Municipal Museum of Ethnology, Cologne, West Germany.

In the author's opinion it is a ritualistic canoe associated with burial and originally made to hold a corpse on dry land, therefore not necessarily made to float on water. The sternpost (182) and prow (176) are of a type which suggest they are from similar small canoes, and the relationship of canoes and bone chests is commented on. See page 101.

184 ⇦
Short club (*patu*) of schist worked into the form of a bird, with overlaid "brow ridge" set below the grip. *Collection:* Auckland Institute and Museum.

This club is from New Zealand's outlying Chatham Islands which were settled by Maoris who assumed the local name of Moriori. The forms of Moriori carving are Archaic in the sense in which this adjective is defined in the Introduction. Moriori carvings sometimes indicate the nature of Classic Maori motifs and it is here proposed that classic *wahaika* (e.g. 185, 186) are best interpreted in the light of Chatham Island *patu* of avian form (such as is seen in this typical specimen).

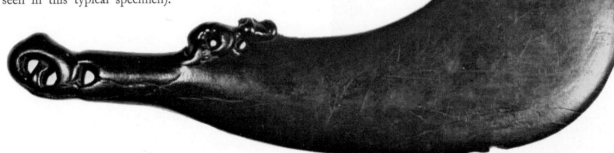

185
Hardwood club of *wahaika* type regularly found in classic Maori collections. *Length:* 17″ (43cm). K. A. Webster *Collection.*

Its relationship to (184), and manaia pommel to bird-head is obvious. The human elements' grip of this specimen correlate with the "brow ridges" on the Moriori club (184), thus again relating Maori and Moriori forms.

186 ·
This unique version of the *wahaika*-type short club appears to be of similar derivation to (185) in its relation to the Moriori club (184). *Length:* 15″ (38cm). Originally illustrated in the engraved plates to *Voyages of Captain Cook* this fine *patu* was presented to the Dominion Museum by K. A. Webster after he had recovered it from obscurity by discovering it in a small antique dealer's shop. The dealer could not identify it but Mr Webster knew immediately it was the *wahaika* illustrated in the plates to *Cook's Voyages*. The clinching feature is a knot·imperfection which may be seen in the original engraving.

A *wahaika*-type short club of late 19th century vintage with skilful but excessive surface decoration. *Length:* 17¼" (44 cm). *Collection:* Dominion Museum, Wellington.

The deep indentations which are usually referred to as "sinuses", after the botanical term for the curve space between lobes of a leaf, probably originated as decorative elaborations of the drilled tie-holes, such as are found on certain old weapons. There is one such tie-knot placed at the end of the Cook *wahaika*, (186), which is typical of the tie-points used to attach feather bundles. Such small feather bundles helped to distract the eye of an opponent when sparring for an opening for the deadly thrust.

187 ⇧
A *wahaika*-type short club from the Wanganui district. *Length:* 14½" (37cm). *Collection:* Dominion Museum, Wellington.

This is a rare example of an old specimen with a surface decorated blade. When surface decoration is found, a flat *patu* is usually of a period when it no longer functioned in fighting; also, elaborate ornament encouraged the average buyer. However this early *patu* (21) has a decorated blade, which confirms the suggestion that short clubs with decorated blades are not confined entirely to the lake era of Maori carving which was so much stimulated by the tourist market.

191 ⇨

A scene from the Maori-Pakeha war in the Bay of Plenty, which ended with the fall of Gate Pa in 1864, sketched on the spot by Lieutenant (later Major General) Horatio Gordon Robley of the 68th Tauranga Regiment. This watercolour depicts the fighting canoe *Hine-tapu* at Christmas time, 1864. Robley noted on the back that he sketched this just fifty years after the first Christian sermon was preached by the Rev Samuel Marsden at the Bay of Islands. This sketch and (192) are in the Dominion Museum, Wellington.

192 ⇨

A sketch by Horatio Gordon Robley of a party of warriors performing a war dance with flourish of wooden weapons, trade tomahawks, and muskets. The place is at a gate of Maketu Pa, Bay of Plenty, 1864.

189 ⇦

The lower end of a long club (*taiaha*) composed of two masks which share a single tongue. *Length of head:* 8⅝″ (22cm). *Collection:* Cambridge University Museum of Archaeology and Ethnology, Cambridge, England. Collected by Capt. James Cook on his first voyage to the Pacific.

⇨ **190**

The *taiaha* is primarily a deadly sword-club, and not a spear as depicted by many artists and movie-makers, and believed by a multitude of native-born New Zealanders. The *taiaha* is one of a class of the flat spatulate blade weapons used for striking which was widely favoured in Polynesia. The tongue at the lower end was used as a kind of prodder, but that end was essentially the ornamental and symbolical part of the *taiaha*. This photograph shows *taiaha* fighters practising their skills at Parihaka, Gisborne, late in the 19th century.

WEAPONS

140

⟡ 193
A war dance by men with paddles, long clubs, muskets and other weapons, at Ohinemutu pa, Lake Rotorua, as seen by English artist George French Angas early in the 1840s. The lithograph is from *The New Zealanders Illustrated*, London, 1846. The author has seen in museums a number of old light-wood paddles with blades painted with rafter-pattern design which appear to have been intended exclusively for dance use. The dance paddle as a distinct artifact is known in many parts of the Pacific.

⟡ 194
A modern haka, with audience of attractive girls, in a performance before the meeting-house at Ohau Channel, Lake Rotorua. The participants are members of the Maori Youth Club who recapture some of the verve of their ancestors, the Ngati-Pikiau people, Te Arawa, Bay of Plenty. The intention of these young Maori people is admirable, but the harsh glossy red paint that is seen on the house detracts from the carvings (for example compare this harsh red with old *kokowai*, e.g. 129). Fortunately red paint tends to fade quickly.

⟡ 195
Wooden bludgeon (*patuki*) of diamond cross-section with its four faces surface-decorated. *Length:* 17″ (43cm). K. A. Webster *Collection.*

Bludgeons termed *patuki* differ from the flat hand-clubs (such as the *wahaika,* 184, 185) as they are true clubs used for delivering in crushing blows and not the slicing and thrusting attacks of flat *patu. Patuki* are found in old collections. They exhibit a variety of cross-sections, namely, round, oval, diagonal, square, oblong. They are typically richly surface-carved in a diversity of decorative styles. With the decline of warfare this weapon appears to have fallen into disfavour in the mid-19th century. It rarely appears in collections made in New Zealand in later periods but is found in abundance in the K. A. Webster and W. O. Oldman Collections which were formed in England from old resources.

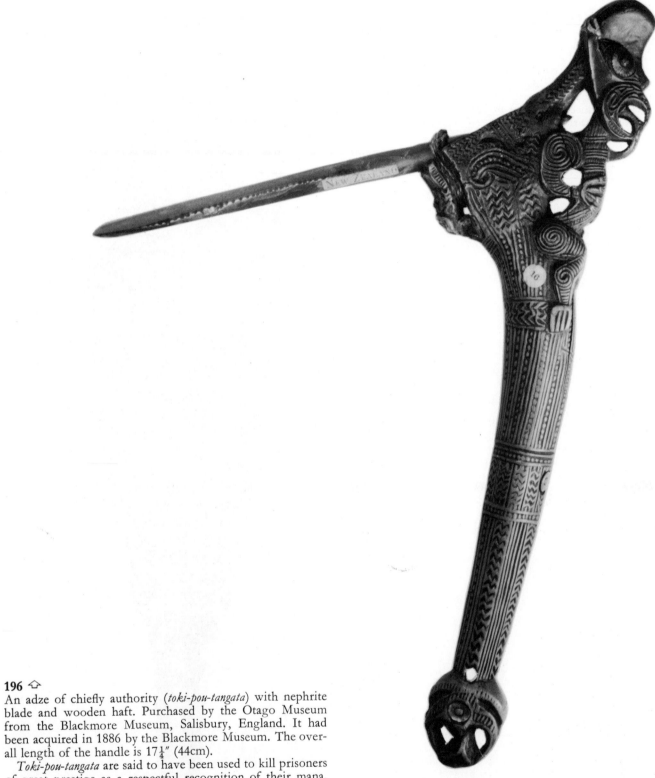

196 ⇧
An adze of chiefly authority (*toki-pou-tangata*) with nephrite
blade and wooden haft. Purchased by the Otago Museum
from the Blackmore Museum, Salisbury, England. It had
been acquired in 1886 by the Blackmore Museum. The overall length of the handle is 17¼" (44cm).

   Toki-pou-tangata are said to have been used to kill prisoners
of great prestige as a respectful recognition of their mana.
Whether this is true or not is an open question. Throughout
Polynesia the adze was often regarded as the abiding place of
a spirit and it sometimes served as a symbol of a god. In New
Zealand the *toki-pou-tangata* certainly served as a mace of
authority and as a baton used in chiefly oratory. Ancestral
images are sometimes portrayed holding a *toki-pou-tangata,* as
in Te Hau-ki-Turanga (102, 106).

197-198 ⇧ ⇧
Side and front view of a baton of uncertain but probably ritualistic use, with handgrip below the image. *Height overall:* 17¼″ (44cm), image, 10⅞″ (25cm). *Collection:* Auckland Institute and Museum, Auckland.

199 ⇧
Baton of type related to (197–198), comprising head above hand shaft with a penis termination at lower end. *Length overall:* 13⅜″ (34cm), head, 4¾″ (12cm). This specimen was recovered from a drain at Te Puke, about 1960.

As with (197, 198) its non-functional form also suggests symbolical use and magical intention.

143

200 ⬧

Comb of classic type with manaia head and inset shell eye. *Height:* 4¾″ (12cm). *Collection:* Cambridge University Museum of Archaeology and Ethnology, Cambridge.

A number of similar combs were collected on the voyages of Cook and by others who visited New Zealand in early historic times. Prehistoric combs of related form were recovered in large numbers from Kauri Point excavations (see captions and specimens, 20, 67), and these help us to explain the shape of the Historic type illustrated here (200). The point of comparison is simply that the older specimen of this type, of which (67) is a beautiful example, corresponds in parts to explain the shape of the late classic type (200) i.e., the high dome of (200) is seen to be a tiki head through comparison with (67), while the nose manaia of the latter explains the manaia of (200) (it is a vestigial "nose").

201-202-203 ⬦

Three views of an ancestral pendant with a suspension-hole drilled into the back of the head. *Dimensions:* 9⅝″ (24.5cm) × 4⅞″ (12.5cm). *Collection:* British Museum, London.

This unusual small tiki corresponds so closely with the well-known nephrite *hei-tiki* of the Maori it is reasonable to regard it as a wooden *hei-tiki* to be worn about the neck. Small tiki pendants carved in wood are known from Easter Island, an island with a culture closely related to that of New Zealand, but this Maori specimen may be unique.

204 ⇧

A watercolour by Augustus Earle (see biographical note to caption 153). Originally reproduced in Earle's *Narrative of a Nine Months' Residence in New Zealand in 1827*, London, 1832, this sketch illustrates a group of Bay of Islands Maori relaxing on the ground before a storehouse. They watch an animated dance of their companions. Music and dance served not only as a leisure-time activity but also as a means of preserving tribal traditions, and a way of cultivating the fighting spirit which was so vital to tribal survival. Small wooden flutes were used for personal enjoyment, especially by young chiefs who courted noble maidens in the face of fierce competition.

205 ⇩

Flute (*koauau*) of phallic design decorated by long rolling spirals which are of North Auckland form. There are three musical stops on the side opposite the neck-cord suspension hole. *Dimensions:* 7″ (17.7cm) × 1¾″ (4.5cm). *Collection:* British Museum, London.

According to museum records of 1915 this flute was "collected in New Zealand at least one hundred years ago", that is, about 1815. The masterly precision of Maori spiral cutting is not surpassed elsewhere in the Pacific and it is one of the special achievements of New Zealand craftsmen.

145

206 ⇕
A long flute (*putorino*), made from two halves exactly fitted together and bound with aerial roots of the *kiekie* vine. *Length:* 15″ (38cm). *Collection:* British Museum, London.

207 ⇔
A small flute of delicate form of the type termed *nguru* carved from a solid piece of wood. *Length:* 4⅜″ (11cm). Sir Walter Buller Collection, Dominion Museum, Wellington.

It was collected on the Wellington west coast in Ngati-Raukawa territory in the 19th century. Three musical stops are drilled into the body of the flute in which a suspension-hole to accommodate a neck-cord is formed by two angled holes drilled from the surface.

⇧
208-209-210

Three views of a massive one-piece flute of *koauau* type of probable North Auckland provenience. *Length:* 8″ (20cm). W. O. Oldman *Collection*, Dominion Museum, Wellington.

Three note-stops are provided on the side opposite the two ancestral images. The side, seen as (209), appears to be in an unfinished stage. Also seen from a side viewing is a hole, below the neck of the upper image, which is intended to take the suspension cord. As with (205), the basic form is phallic, both ends terminating as glans penis which are also abstracted as heads with discernible eye and nose features.

147

211 ↶
A puppet (*karetao*) with movable arms, commonly termed a Maori "jumping jack". Height: 14½″ (37cm). K. A. Webster *Collection*.

Delightful puppet figures were controlled mainly by shaking the figure from the hand-grip base (cut off in this specimen, compare 216). By shaking the *karetao* and at the same time tightening or loosening the arm cords it assumed various postures. *Karetao* served as a kind of theatrical prop to aid a performer who chanted as the stances of the puppet were skilfully manipulated. A feature of this figure is the flintlock musket engraved on the left arm.

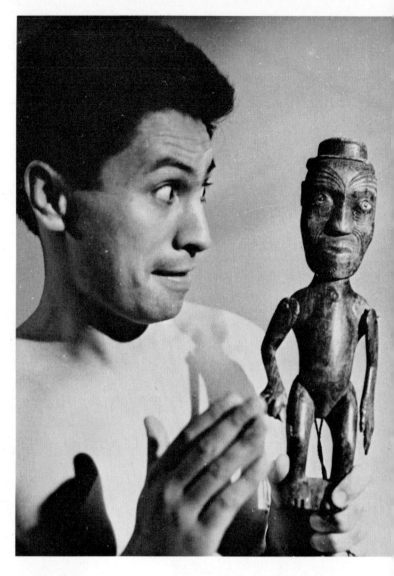

212 ↶
In this photograph, taken by the author in 1964, shows Mr Ratu Tibble of Te Aroha operating the puppet illustrated (211). Ratu responds with his face and body to movements of the puppet which he is partly controlling. In former times a puppet song (*oriori-karetao*) was chanted, but this art is virtually lost. It has a promising prospect of revival through the collaboration of carvers, entertainers, researchers into Maori music, and through the response of New Zealanders and visitors seeking something of the old Maori traditions.

213 ↷
Games played an important role in Maori life. Some required carved objects, or structural equipment such as this swing seen at Taupo by George French Angas about 1844. The lithograph is from *The New Zealanders Illustrated*, London, 1846.

EQUIPMENT OF GAMES

149

◁ **214**
New Zealand village life, although harassed by inter-tribal fighting, had its seasons of leisure made possible by a rich land and a well-developed Polynesian gardening and food-gathering economy. In this scene, sketched by George French Angas for *The New Zealanders Illustrated*, London, 1846, tribal relatives of the Taranaki district meet with customary nose-pressing (*hongi*). The background includes a village storehouse, a dwelling house, and majestical Mount Egmont, symbol of Taranaki.

◁ **215**
The grandeur of scenery in the central lakes district of the North Island and the sophisticated Maori life made possible by wood crafts and many other skills, is admirably represented by this scene from *The New Zealanders Illustrated*, London, 1846. The foreground here shows canoes, while on the far side of Lake RotoAira stands the fortified village of Motupoi. The mountain backdrop includes Mounts Tongariro, Ngauruhoe, and Ruapehu.

⇨ **216**
Puppet or "jumping jack" (*karetao*) cut from a dense hardwood and engraved with tattoo lines on both face and buttocks. *Overall height:* 20¾″ (52.7 cm), *image:* 17¾″ (45cm). This example, which has the quality usually found only in the earliest woodcarving, was returned to New Zealand in 1948. W. O. Oldman *Collection,* Dominion Museum, Wellington.

◊ **217** (detail of end figure **218**) ↷
Whiplash stick (*kotaha*). *Length overall:* 38¼″ (97cm), *image,*
4¼″ (10.7cm). K. A. Webster *Collection.*

A favourite Maori sport was a game in which small javelins
or darts (*teka*) of wood were cast by competitive players who
shot only for distance. The darts were first lightly thrust into
the ground then caught by slip-knot in a cord which was
attached to the player's whiplash (*kotaha*). The lower end of
the *kotaha* was notched for the attachment of a cord while the
upper end had an image of somewhat comical type. The detail
(218) shows the typical *kotaha* figure with its large masklike
face, arms clutching body, buttocks out-thrust in a tensed
posture, with feet placed behind the lower part of the face.

Treasure-boxes (*waka-huia, papa-huia,* or *papa-hou*) are notably of very varied style, ingenious in form and design, and typically of fine craftsmanship. As they were commonly of portable size and elaborately carved they were much sought after by early visitors who took them home as curios. How so many Maoris were persuaded to part with such valuable and personal possessions is hard to understand, yet the number of fine boxes in the museums of a dozen countries would amount to a remarkable total. Some of the best boxes were returned to New Zealand in the W. O. Oldman and the K. A. Webster Collections.

It is generally held that *waka-huia* were made in leisure time by men who were not professional woodcarvers. As most men carved after a fashion and time was not pressing, many of these boxes emerged from personal skill and abundant leisure. The name *waka-huia* has given rise to the notion they were used exclusively for feathers, especially the storage of the prized black-and-white tail feathers of the *huia*; however, *huia* may mean "anything much prized", and it seems certain that jade ornaments, combs, small chisels, and other small and tapu possessions ranked equal with or above feather ornaments as personal possessions. Any precious object including small weapons might be placed in *waka-huia*.

It is difficult to appreciate the designs on these boxes by studying photographs, as the compositions extend around all four sides and ends. The boxes were designed to hang from rafters, and the concentration of surface decoration tends to be on the underside as the boxes were most often seen from below. Probably for this reason the undersides were usually finished first, and indeed the underside is the part usually complete in unfinished boxes. The lid and sides are sometimes found with unfinished areas, as is seen in the box (89, 92).

219 ⬁

The underside of a treasure-box (*waka-huia*) a portion of which appears in enlargement as (72). *Length:* 23″ (68cm). From Cook's voyages. *Collection:* British Museum, London.

The usual style of surface decoration utilises certain basic elements, namely dog-tooth notches (*pakati*) between parallel ridges (*haehae*), thus forming the simplest pattern of the *rauponga* type. Manaia types are best observed in the enlarged detail, (72).

220 ⬂

Underside of a treasure-box (*waka-huia*) of North Auckland type. *Length:* 29″ (74cm). *Collection:* University Museum, University of Pennsylvania, USA.

This singularly beautiful box may be related to the three Auckland boxes of equal quality, (221, 222, 223). The specific *waka-huia* style of the northern boxes combines oblong form, long rolling spirals, snakelike out-turned manaia, and images with high-domed heads and sinuous bodies set in low relief. These figures are elaborated to such an extreme extent, and often so merge into the general pattern, that it is difficult to isolate component elements. Some of these images appear to represent *marakihau* (see pages 50–53, and boxes 221–223).

221 ⇦
Underside of a treasure-box (*waka-huia*) of northern type, with a manaia head missing from one end. *Dimensions:* 23″ (58cm) × 5″ (13cm) × 3″ (7.5cm). W. O. Oldman *Collection,* Dominion Museum, Wellington.

This box formerly belonged to Sir James Cotter of Cork, who said that it was brought back to Ireland by a member of his family several generations ago.

222 ⇩
Underside of a treasure-box (*waka-huia*) which was presented to Rev Samuel Marsden by a Bay of Island Maori chief early in the 19th century. *Dimensions:* 24⅜″ (62cm) × 8⅝″ (22cm) × 2″ (5cm). This box was first seen by the author at the exhibition entitled "Cook and a Hundred Years After" held at New Zealand House, London, in June 1956. On that occasion it was lent for public viewing by a descendant of Samuel Marsden and later the same box was exhibited for a period at the Dominion Museum, Wellington, and elsewhere in New Zealand.

223 ⇦
Underside of a treasure-box (*waka-huia*) of North Auckland style. *Dimensions:* 21″ (53cm) × 6½″ (16.5cm) × 3¼″ (8.3cm).

224 ⇧
Lid from a treasure-box with single image. *Length:* 15" (38 cm), image, 8¼" (21cm). W. O. Oldman *Collection,* Hawke's Bay Museum, Napier.

It is probable that the plain surface around the image which gives this lid such an appeal to the modern eye, is merely an unfinished area.

226 ⇩
A view of the underside of a treasure-box (*waka-huia*) of a design based on two tiki placed end to end and probably performing in the male and female role of (225). *Length:* 17" (43cm). *Collection:* Frobenius Institute, Frankfurt-on-Main, West Germany.

225 ⇧
Lid from a treasure-box of probable East Coast provenience. *Length:* 16" (41cm). W. O. Oldman *Collection,* Hawke's Bay Museum, Napier.

The design on this lid is composed of three images, the upper pair being in sexual connection although slightly severed—"censored" with a knife by some idiot. The theme of sexual intercourse is common on the lids of treasure-boxes (compare this box lid with 231).

☝
227-228-229

Three views of a large treasure-box (*waka-huia*). Side view (227), view of lid when removed from box (228), and view of underside (229). An East Coast provenience seems probable for this fine box. *Dimensions: length:* 29⅜" (74cm) × 8¼" (21 cm) × 5½" (14cm). *Collection:* Cambridge University Museum of Archaeology and Ethnology, Cambridge.

This box was purchased in London in 1886 and is believed to have been used to hold personal treasures such as nephrite clubs of war (*patu-pounamu*) and other short weapons and rare things of substantial size. The lid has strong sexual elements including the copulating figures (231), and it compares well with the theme of lid (225). By being virtually finished on the lid but unfinished below and on the sides it infringes the general rule of procedure in secondary surface decoration on *waka-huia* as discussed on page 73, namely that craftsmen worked first on the underside (following the formation of the basic box) because this was the part normally seen by those sitting or lying in a house when the box was suspended from a rafter.

⇧
230-231-232

Three views of a large treasure-box (*waka-huia*) side view (230), view of lid removed from box (231), and view of underside (232). *Dimensions: length, 34″ (86cm). Collection:* Auckland Institute and Museum, Auckland.

This box, which related in size and type to the *waka-huia* (227–229), appears also shares an East Coast provenience. A special feature of this box is the pair of three-dimensional images on the top which serve as a handle when the lid is lifted.

233 ⬆

An image of East Coast type from a feather-box (*waka-huia*).
This box in the collection of the Pitt Rivers Museum, Oxford,
has this vigorous small image on the lid.

The tiki embodies the typical characteristics of the image
type often seen in Classic Maori wood sculpture, and, although
vastly different in size it compares in conception and style
with the image from Te Hau-ki-Turanga which appears as the
frontispiece to this book.

ILLUSTRATIONS

BIBLIOGRAPHY

This is a list of works mentioned in the text, and specific papers or books used but not quoted. A number of standard titles helpful in reading for a general background knowledge of Classical Maori culture are included. Readers who wish to study Maori carving intensively may turn to the numerous references under the New Zealand section and classified headings in C. R. H. Taylor's *A Pacific Bibliography* (second edition, Clarendon Press, Oxford, 1965). The excellent three-volume *An Encyclopaedia of New Zealand*, edited by A. H. McLintock and published in Wellington by the Government Printer in 1966, has a wealth of articles relating to Maori wood sculpture (e.g., information on totara, nephrite and Maori social customs etc.). The contribution on Maori art by J. M. McEwen in the second volume includes an illustrated summary of carving style areas of New Zealand.

Archey, G., *South Sea Folk: Handbook of Maori and Oceanic Ethnology*, (2nd ed.), Auckland War Memorial Museum, Auckland, 1949.

Archey, G., Miscellaneous carving papers in the Records of the Auckland Institute and Museum: *Wood carving in the North Auckland area* (1933); *Taurapa* (1938); *Tauihu* (1956); *Tiki and pou* (1958); *Pare of human figure construction* (1960); *Spiral-dominated composition in pare* (1962); *Maori wood sculpture: the human head and face* (1967).

Archey, G., *Sculpture and Design: an outline of Maori art*, Handbook of the Auckland War Memorial Museum, Auckland, 1955.

Archey, G., "The Art Forms of Polynesia", *Bulletin of the Auckland Institute and Museum* No. 4, Auckland, 1965.

Badner, M., "The Protruding Tongue and Related Motifs in the Art Styles of the American Northwest Coast, New Zealand and China", in *Two Studies of Art in the Pacific Area*, Vienna, 1966.

Barrow, T., "Free-standing Maori Images", in *Anthropology in the South Seas* (a volume of essays in honour of H. D. Skinner), pp. 111–120, New Plymouth, 1959.

Barrow, T., "Maori Godsticks collected by the Rev Richard Taylor", *Dominion Museum Records in Ethnology*, vol. 1, no. 5, Wellington, 1959.

Barrow, T., "Maori Godsticks in Various Collections", *Dominion Museum Records in Ethnology*, vol. 1, no. 5, Wellington, 1961.

Barrow, T., *The Life and Work of the Maori Carver*, a secondary school bulletin published by the School Publications Branch, Department of Education, Wellington, 1963.

Barrow, T., *The Decorative Arts of the New Zealand Maori*, A. H. & A. W. Reed, Wellington, 1964.

Barrow, T., *A Guide to the Maori Meeting House Te Hau-ki-Turanga*, Dominion Museum, Wellington, 1965.

Barrow, T., "Material Evidence of the Bird-man concept in Polynesia", paper pp. 191–213 in *Polynesian Culture History: Essays in Honour of Kenneth P. Emory*, Bernice P. Bishop Museum Special Publication 56, Honolulu, 1967.

Best, E., "Maori storehouses and kindred structures", Part I, *Dominion Museum Bulletin* no. 5, Wellington, 1915.

Best, E., "Notes on the Occurrence of the Lizard in Maori Carvings", *N.Z. Journal of Science and Technology*, vol. 5, pp. 231–235, Wellington, 1923.

Best, E., "The Maori Canoe", *Dominion Museum Bulletin* no. 7, Wellington, 1925.

Best, E., *The Maori* (2 vols.) Memoir Vol. 5 of the Polynesian Society, for the Board of Maori Ethnological Research, Wellington, 1924.

Best, E., "Games and pastimes of the Maori", *Dominion Museum Bulletin* no. 8, Wellington, 1925.

Best, E., "The Maori Pa", *Dominion Museum Bulletin* no. 6, Wellington, 1927.

Buck, Sir Peter (Te Rangi Hiroa), *The Coming of the Maori* (second edition), Maori Purposes Fund Board and Whitcombe & Tombs, Christchurch, 1950.

Buhler, A., Barrow, T., and Mountford, C. P., *Oceania and Australia:* "The art of the South Seas"; pp. 191–206, *The art of the New Zealand Maori* by Barrow, Methuen, London, 1962.

Cook's Voyages. Of the many editions *The Journals of Captain James Cook on his Voyages of Discovery*, (4 vols), edited from the original manuscripts by H. C. Beaglehole for the Hakluyt Society, is the most complete, authoritative and standard. Printed at the Cambridge University Press for the Hakluyt Society, 1955–1967.

Cranstone, B. A. L., "Ancient Maori Bone Chest", *British Museum Quarterly*, 17, pp. 58–59, London, 1953.

Dodge, E. S., *The New Zealand Maori collection in the Peabody Museum of Salem*, Peabody Museum, Salem, 1941.

Downes, T. W., "Old Native Stone-cut Artifacts from Waverley", *Journal of the Polynesian Society*, vol. 41, pp. 50–58 and 312–316, New Plymouth, 1932.

Earle, A., *Narrative of a nine months' residence in New Zealand in 1827*, Longman, London, 1832.

Edge-Partington, J., "Maori Burial Chests (*Atamira* or *Tupa-Pakau*)", *Man*, art. 18, London, 1909.

Firth, R. W., "The Maori Carver", *Journal of the Polynesian Society*, vol. 34, pp. 277–291, New Plymouth, 1925.

Hamilton, A., *Maori Art, the art workmanship of the Maori Race in New Zealand*, Dunedin, 1896.

Heine-Geldern, R., "A Note on Relations between the Art Styles of the Maori and of Ancient China", in *Two Studies of Art in the Pacific Area*, Vienna, 1966.

Houston, J., "A Taranaki lintel", *Journal of the Polynesian Society*, vol. 68, pp. 239–240, New Plymouth, 1959.

Mair, G., "The Building of Hotunui, Whare Whakairo, W. H. Taipari's Carved House at Thames, 1878 (told by

Mereana Mokomoko, widow of the late chief, W. H. Taipari, To Gilbert Mair, 12th July, 1897)", *Transactions of the New Zealand Institute*, vol. 30, pp. 41–44, 1898.

McEwen, J. M., Article "Maori Art" in *An Encyclopaedia of New Zealand*, vol. 2, pp. 408–429, Government Printer, Wellington, 1966.

Mead, S. M., *The Art of Maori Carving,* A. H. & A. W. Reed, Wellington, 1961.

Ngata, Sir Apirana T., "The Origin of Maori Carving", *Te Ao Hou*, nos. 22 and 23, Wellington, 1958.

Oldman, W. O., "Skilled Handwork of the Maori: being the Oldman Collection of Artifacts illustrated and described", *Memoirs of the Polynesian Society*, vol. 14, Wellington, 1946.

Phillipps, W. J., *Maori Carving*, Thomas Avery, New Plymouth, 1941.

Phillipps, W. J., "Carved Maori Houses of the Eastern Districts of the North Island", *Records of the Dominion Museum,* pp. 69–119, Wellington, 1944.

Phillipps, W. J., "Carved Houses of Te Arawa", *Dominion Museum Records in Ethnology*, Vol. 1, no. 1, Wellington, 1946.

Phillipps, W. J., "Maori Houses and Food Stores", *Dominion Museum Monograph* no. 8, Wellington, 1952.

Phillipps, W. J., "Carved Maori Houses of Western and Northern Areas of New Zealand", *Dominion Museum Monograph* no. 9, Wellington, 1955.

Phillipps, W. J., *Maori Carving Illustrated*, A. H. & A. W. Reed, Wellington, 1955.

Robley, H. G., *Moko or Maori tattooing*, Chapman & Hall, London, 1896.

Schuster, C., "Joint Marks: a possible index of cultural contact between America, Oceania and the Far East", *Royal Tropical Institute*, no. XCIV *Physical Anthropology* no. 39, Amsterdam, 1951.

Skinner, H. D., "The Origin and Relationship of Maori Material Culture and Decorative Art", *Journal of the Polynesian Society*, vol. 33, pp. 229–243. New Plymouth, 1924.

Skinner, H. D., "Crocodile and Lizard in New Zealand Myth and Material Culture", *Records of the Otago Museum,* Dunedin, 1964.

Shawcross, W., "An Archaeological Assemblage of Maori Combs", *Journal of the Polynesian Society*, vol. 73, pp. 382–398, Wellington, 1964.

Stevenson, A. G., "Maori Wooden Bowls", *Records of the Auckland Institute and Museum,* vol. 2, no. 4, Auckland, 1939.

Taiapa, P., "The Art of Adzing—as taught by Eramiha Kapua, of the Ngati Tarawhai, Te Arawa, to students of the Maori Arts and Crafts School, Rotorua", *Te Ao Hou,* no. 33, 1960.

Wardwell, A., *The Sculpture of Polynesia*, The Art Institute of Chicago, 1967.

Webster, K. A., *The Armytage Collection of Maori Jade,* Cable Press, London, 1948.

Williams, H. W., "The Maori Whare; Construction of a Maori house", *Journal of the Polynesian Society*, vol. 5, pp. 144–145, New Plymouth, 1896.

Williams, H. W., *A Dictionary of the Maori Language*, (sixth edition), Government Printer, Wellington, *1957*.

Willitt, F., *A Maori store-chamber slab in the Manchester Museum*, Manchester, art., 197, 1955.

INDEX

Figures in italic refer to illustrations or captions

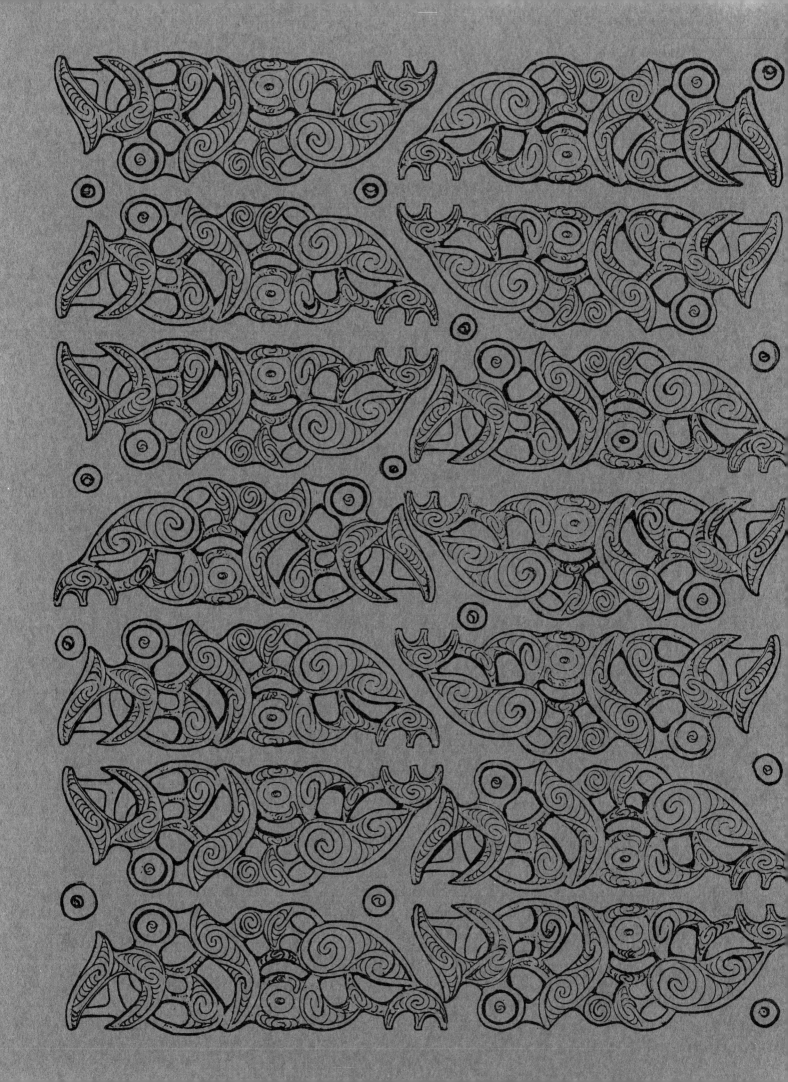